The Postmodern University

THE POSTMODERN UNIVERSITY:
Essays on the Deconstruction of the Humanities

Stanley Fogel

ECW PRESS

CANADIAN CATALOGUING IN PUBLICATION DATA

Fogel, Stanley.

The postmodern university

ISBN 1-55022-005-5 (bound) –
ISBN 1-55022-004-7 (pbk.)

1. Deconstruction.   2. Humanities.   3. Universities
and colleges.   I. Title.

PN98.D43F63 1988   801'.95   C87-093336-1

Published with the assistance of St. Jerome's College, Waterloo, Ontario. Additional grants have been provided by the
Ontario Arts Council and The Canada Council.

Designed and typeset by ECW Production Services, Oakville,
Ontario. Cover artwork by Bette Davies. Printed and bound
by University of Toronto Press, Downsview, Ontario.

Published by ECW PRESS, 307 Coxwell Avenue, Toronto,
Ontario M4L 3B5

Table of Contents

ACKNOWLEDGEMENTS

Some chapters of this book have appeared previously in various journals. They are as follows:

- "Gobble, Gobble, Gobble: Critical Appetites," *The Canadian Review of American Studies* (Winter 1984).
- "The Importance of Being Earnest: Literary Critics in America," *The Canadian Review of American Studies* (Spring 1986).
- "Palinodes and Palindromes," *International Fiction Review* (Winter 1984).
- "The Ludic Temperament of John Barth," *Fantasy Newsletter* (July 1982).
- "Travels With My Cant," *2 Plus 2* (1985).

Thanks again to Laura Moyer for transforming my longhand into lucidity (?).

"Michel Foucault's Touchstones" was written in collaboration with Susan Gray.

This book is for anyone who has sat sceptically through lectures delivered assuredly on such topics as literature, composition, history, philosophy . . . .

Introduction

In "Marriage and Love" Emma Goldman, sanely and disdainfully, it seems to me, summarizes marriage thusly:

> Marriage and love have nothing in common; they are as far apart as the poles; are, in fact, antagonistic to each other. No doubt some marriages have been the result of love. Not, however, because love could assert itself only in marriage; much rather is it because few people can completely outgrow a convention. . . . At any rate, while it is true that some marriages are based on love, and while it is equally true that in some cases love continues in married life, I maintain that it does so regardless of marriage, and not because of it.[1]

Lovers desirous of an institutional framework, some external sanctioning of their commitment, intrepidly and heedlessly ignore her assessment. So, too, with those enamoured of learning, of intellectual inquiry. The institution, the university, manifests itself for the most part as a static, hierarchized expression of a powerful urge, yet its endurance and occasional vitality as learning's nexus are incontestable.

The essays contained herein seek to explore the ways the university contains and shapes thinkers' queries into and discoveries in the humanities. My perspective is probably that of an iconoclast testing the boundaries of the humanities, examining what is and is not said or written and how material is and is not taught. One need only submit proposals to the

---

[1] Emma Goldman, "Marriage and Love," in *Anarchism and Other Essays*, 3rd. rev. ed. (New York: Mother Earth Publishing Association, 1917), p. 233.

Canadian Federation for the Humanities or examine the curricula of graduate schools of English in Canada to see how rigid and stylized a potentially anarchistic activity has become; thus, many of these essays are provocative and confrontational. They are products of a scorn developed as a result of the way the humanities are husbanded (*touché*) by Canadian academics. (William Gass's sentiment that he wants to rise so high that when he shits he won't miss anybody is perhaps apposite here.)

This book is divided into four sections: theory, literature, culture, conclusion. The essays grouped in the theory section have the broadest focus, their purview being the organization of the humanities, the situation of academics who teach in that area, the notion of the classics, and the responses of students to literature and their situation, among other issues. The essays that deal with literature scrutinize how the concept "literature" has developed, how critics operate on and maintain it, how postmodern literature and theory disrupt traditional perceptions of the discipline. Although two of these essays first appeared as omnibus reviews, the questions raised in them make them, I hope, seminal in a context beyond that of the specific books reviewed. Also, although the occasional quotation appears more than once throughout the course of this book, it does not, I think, detract from the cumulative reading of all the essays published here. The brief culture section may be seen as providing a respite from the academic concerns engaged in the other three sections. It contains a number of belle-lettristic pieces in which, if it is not too portentous to say so, someone with a postmodern sensibility assesses, among other things, the concepts of love, travel, photography, sex, and consumerism. The conclusion provides a definition of the contentious term, postmodernism.

To say of an academic book that it is not for everyone is surely a pleonasm. Nonetheless, even within the university ghetto the book will have its detractors, to wit M. Gilbert Porter who wrote the following letter to the editors of *The Canadian Review of American Studies* in response to one of these essays:

I have just received a copy of the bitchy little piece of deconstructionist drivel by Stanley Fogel that is supposed to be a review of my book *The Art of Grit*.... Gentlefolk, this will never do. I can abide a negative review if it bears some relation to my work and if it is carefully reasoned. This "review," however, has nothing to do with my treatment of Ken Kesey's fiction and even less to do with responsible literary criticism. It is unorganized, distorted, pretentious, self indulgent, badly written, and silly. In short, Fogel is as full of shit as a Christmas turkey, and you are guilty of egregious editorial misjudgment to publish such effete nonsense as serious literary commentary. I know nothing of your journal, but I think I can predict with confidence that it will be short lived if it continues to include superficial simpery of the Fogel stripe.[1]

Despite the experimental nature of some of the pieces contained herein, no "scratch-and-sniff" remedy for apoplexy is appended. The complacency of the academy – comfortable with the framework of knowledge – is my target. *Caveat emptor.*

---

[1] "Reasoning Together," *The Canadian Review of American Studies*, 16 (1985), 251.

THEORY

Intellectual Enemas

"No one achieves frivolity straight off. It is a privilege and an art; it is the pursuit of the superficial by those who, having discerned the impossiblity of any certitude, have conceived a disgust for such things . . . ."

– E.M. Cioran, *A Short History of Decay*

Consider this (call it "Anecdote of the Gyr-ations"): I have always been a recusant, balking especially at the avuncular image of the professor dispensing wisdom from behind a pipe the way baseball pitchers throw fastballs while their cheeks are wadded with chewing tobacco. Moreover, I don't much like, and never have liked, the power academics have to define their disciplines (what is or is not hallowed literature? what are or are not the hierarchies of genres, periods, authors?), dictate to their students, and pass themselves off as experts in their society. I could tell the story of organizing a committee of graduate students to investigate a tenure committee's decision; however, I would probably sound like Jerry Farber in "The Student As Nigger" haranguing university administrations and championing student power. While my sentiments lie strongly with Farber (so strongly I would rather not write his coda and besides, it is a simple forceful cry that requires only direct action, an assault on the edifices which control and dispense knowledge), I have more convoluted measures vis-à-vis the academy which I wish to explore and articulate. Regardless, agitating against the role of the academic (and its connotations of sobriety and wisdom, about which more later), I was moved once (and this is the story I will tell) to accept an offer to perform at a women's "stag," that is, to strip there.

I had received a letter marked "Personal and Confidential," which began "Dear Doctor . . ." and continued in very genteel language to inquire as to whether I would strip on the occasion of a friend's impending marriage. The writer mentioned that an acquaintance of hers had met me at a costume party which I had attended in rather skimpy attire. The woman concluded her missive by providing her phone number and decorous encouragement. There was no wrestling with my conscience and I phoned immediately to accept. The night before my debut I choreographed a routine and coined the name Doc Torrid (Doctor Id). Eschewing any liquor or what Thomas Pynchon has referred to as "indole alkaloids" so that I would be alert to the nuances both of my performance and its reception, I arrived at a pre-arranged side entrance and sneaked downstairs. A dozen or so women were priming themselves by drinking and watching a porno film, oblivious to my presence.

On cue (Rod Stewart's "Do You Think I'm Sexy?") Doc Torrid appeared and proceeded to shed his clothes. As each article of clothing was tossed away a few strategically placed Band-Aids were revealed, each one containing a message (e.g., "men's nipples are sensitive too – demonstrate" and " 'Good taste is acquired censorship' – kiss my ass" – quotations, as we know, are an academic's staple). Audience participation was avid until I was clad only in a G string, whereupon the bride-to-be stepped forward and peeled the Band-Aid which read, "the key to the treasure is fastened to its location, what the guest-of-honour must provide is, one of two, lubrication." Confronted by no G string and the dilemma enunciated above she opted for the less risqué of the two alternatives before wresting the prize – a prophylactic with the fortune-cookie-like inscription, "alas, every phallus is sometimes unreliable, what the guest-of-honour requires is something less pliable." At that point, a dildo was produced as her gift. Doctor Id prepared to abscond, only to be encouraged to linger with the guests who, it was discovered, were convinced of the performer's authenticity.

The reader of this account should hold in abeyance his or her contention that this *jeu d'esprit* has little or nothing to do with the book's focus and the tone of scholarly prose generally and, moreover, that it is either a frippery to sensationalize the more theoretical material to follow or a jejune act equivalent to graduands trading rolls of toilet paper for the degrees they received – something that was popular in the late 1960s and the early 1970s. That, of course, was the time of direct "agitprop" acts, of diatribes such as Farber's and Louis Kampf's when he was president of the Modern Language Association, as well as the more politically engaged assaults on the academy's sanctity that William McGill chronicles in *The Year of the Monkey* – a reminiscence of his embattled days as chancellor of the University of California at San Diego. So look on my own autobiographical tidbit, if you will, as an admission of sympathy with those halcyon days when the university's complacent *status quo* sensibility was threatened. It surely takes no sociological data to realize that today the humanities are for the most part taught – in terms of form and content – with an antiquarian as well as an authoritarian tilt. Some interdisciplinary programs notwithstanding, departments remain the arbiters of knowledge, their established genres, periods, methodologies only modestly altered and revalued over the many years. Also, and especially pernicious, the university apparatus which includes presidents, deans, heads, and the ranked professoriat has not budged at all despite some occasional threats and actions that student activists made and took in the now receding days of protest. Fusty academics, cushioned by their degrees and their *curricula vitae*, are, it should be said, the major and most resistant obstacles to a different internal perception of post-secondary education. (The funding of universities produces a different and, in this case, external target.)

You may also regard my story, to return from my polemical outburst, as a deliberately disruptive beginning to a text, one which marks itself as having an affinity with the most recent confrontation with academic stability, what has been called the deconstructive turn. A more recondite assault on the seemingly inviolable edifices of learning than that of Farber, et al., deconstruction has, nonetheless, brought with it a threat to established notions of education and learning in the humanities. One time at the School of Criticism and Theory at Northwestern University of Evanston, Illinois, E.D. Hirsch, Jr., whose *Validity in Interpretation*, *The Aims of Interpretation*, and the recent (frightfully rearguard and neo-conservative) *Cultural Literacy*, reveal him as committed to orthodox entrees to literary texts, ones which seek valid, discernible unitary meanings, berated Geoffrey Hartman, whose *Saving the Text* and *Criticism in the Wilderness* postulate a less sure mode of critical operations, by waving the Yale University calendar (Hartman is a faculty member at Yale) at him and challenging him to refute the claim that he was not teaching what the calendar outlined as course content. As forcefully as what might be called the anarchist or libertarian attack on university power – and that quarter's denunciation, manned by, among others, Ivan Illich and Paolo Friere, is by no means a feckless one – extrapolators of deconstruction have provided what can be regarded as a more intellectual or theory-oriented assault on the traditional framework of the humanities.

In their beginnings, as in my own perhaps, can be discerned an unorthodox disposition towards scholarly inquiry. In his essay "Living On. Border Lines," to choose at random an opening that calls into question formulaic critical openings, Jacques Derrida breezily begins:

But who's talking about living?
In other words on living?[1]

This time, "in other words" does not put something into other words, does not clarify an ambiguous expression, does not function like an "i.e." Heretofore, critical practice, examination in the humanities, functioned as an "i.e.," an insight into or organization of events, ideas, etc. The researcher wrote "in other words" about his or her investigations, offering some resolution to diverse problems both microcosmic (e.g., the meaning of a poem) or macrocosmic (e.g., the nature of literature). "Living On. Border Lines" not only presents two discrete essays running in a parallel fashion through the pages, as does *Willie Masters' Lonesome Wife*, William Gass's novella in which he mixes three stories in different typographies on each page, but it also immediately questions its own language, advancing not in pellucid prose with linear sequential argumentation but

---

[1] Jacques Derrida, "Living On. Border Lines," trans. James Hulbert in Harold Bloom et al., *Deconstruction and Criticism* (New York: Seabury, 1979), p. 75.

proceeding self-consciously and reflexively. One might have as easily selected Michel Foucault's first sentence in "The Discourse on Language": "I would really like to have slipped imperceptibly into this lecture, as into all the others I shall be delivering, perhaps over the years ahead."[1] Foucault's essay also unsettles at once in that it seems, as does Derrida's piece, to promise something other than explication, interpretation, synthesis. The sense is given that one cannot proffer wisdom in a sectioned, compartmentalized fashion, that language ensnares one as much as delivers one's meaning.

Literary criticism and, indeed, most university discourses and disciplines have, or at least contend that they have, provided meanings, answers, sure disquisitions *about* all manner of physical and metaphysical phenomena. What Derrida and Foucault, as well as their phalanx of acolytes, promise is opacity vis-à-vis language as well as a dismantling of most of the categories, genres, dualities, etc. that have bulwarked traditional studies in the humanities. Rather than language and text being a conduit to the world of knowledge which in some way resides outside of textuality, they get placed in the foreground, becoming the contemporary critic's preoccupation, his or her resistant media. The pedagogue's explanatory prose, devoid of tropes except as embellishment, gives way to the artist's dextrous play with words. Logical, ratiocinative arguments are rejected in favour of such experimental works as Derrida's *Glas*, Hartman's *Saving the Text* or Ihab Hassan's *Paracriticisms* which, like Julio Cortázar's *Hopscotch* with its two distinct schema for reading the novel (one involving progression from chapter to chapter, the other demanding "hopscotching" through the novel), employ unorthodox typographical and layout techniques among more obvious departures from norms that have regulated even the visual perception of texts. Neologisms such as "grammatology" and "differance" and play with names as in Derrida's play with his own signature in "Signature, Event, Context" and his play with the names of Francis Ponge and Jean Genet in other essays – these devices

---

[1] Michel Foucault, "The Discourse on Language," in *The Archaeology of Knowledge*, trans. A.M. Sheridan Smith (New York: Pantheon, 1972), p. 215.

have become central to avant-garde criticism, challenging the notion that the critical text is ancillary to the world, work, or concept being explored. Critical theory currently stresses the contestation of its own parameters, styles, techniques. As Christopher Norris in *Deconstruction: Theory and Practice* and Catherine Belsey in *Critical Practice* have stressed, deconstruction abandons explication. Thus, "Living On. Border Lines" requires a reader willing to be situated on the borders of traditional methods of criticism. Paraphrasing, the *modus operandi* of the so-called new critic, and codifying, the manner of Northrop Frye (as he anatomizes criticism), have become devalued, thought to be reductive, rigidified, or clichéd procedures; by extension, for their most implacable enemies, such activities are thought to be ideological, metaphorical adjuncts of hegemony and totalitarianism. They are considered to be smug and facile appurtenances, reinforcing metaphysical assumptions with their systematizing and explanatory focuses. The unitary meanings they engender falsely simplify texts, collapsing heterodox elements into harmony; in addition, they reduce language's complexity allowing the notion to prevail that it is a tool, a transparent medium.

That deconstruction is not an aberration, some localized response to a critical glut seized on by opportunistic junior English professors, can be demonstrated by its compatibility with the perspective contained in much contemporary art. One can speak of a postmodern sensibility which includes deconstruction as one manifestation of its distinctiveness. The contemporary novel, for instance, as practised by experimental writers such as Donald Barthelme, Robert Coover, Thomas Pynchon, Alain Robbe-Grillet, John Fowles, Robert Kroetsch, and Cortázar, to range widely over the fiction written in many nations and languages, disseminates the same kinds of insights offered by deconstruction: teleology and metaphysics are fabrications; none of the conventions of literature is sacrosanct; language does not mirror or capture reality; realism is disparaged, regarded as a style, and a feckless one at that; meaning, truths, absolutes are revealed as ideological or patently artificial; knowledge is a construct. Concomitantly, contemporary novelists whom we might call postmodern (the former term denoting an historical era, the latter an avant-garde sensibility) engage in legerdemain and ludic exercises, pun obsessively, write palinodes – metaphorically speaking – and in all ways seek to dismantle styles of living and styles of thinking that, they suspect, have become reified, regarded as natural. Among many examples of experimentation there are, for instance, Barth's Moebius strip at the beginning of *Lost in the Funhouse* ("Once upon a time there/was a story that began"), Coover's multiple unresolved story lines in many of the short stories in *Pricksongs & Descants*, the false foreward to Vladimir Nabokov's *Lolita*, Jorge Luis Borges's scholarly codas to nonexistent books, etc. Unlike those who range from optimist to nihilist, from spiritualist to materialist, writers with a postmodern sensibility treat all systems, all ways of seeing the world, as fiction. They are sceptical of all manner of formulations and theories; they might incisively be spoken of as deconstructors themselves, undermining all shibboleths of art and life.

It is, therefore, not difficult to integrate their perspective with the postmodern aesthetic enunciated by Jean-François Lyotard, who defines it as "that which refuses the consolation of good forms, of a consensus of *taste* which would permit the nostalgia of the impossible to be felt in common."[1] That there are archetypes or forms which in some ways facilitate expression of some inarticulate, pre-linguistic essence Lyotard, along with Foucault and Derrida, among many others, rejects outright. Pre-existent genres, inviolable categories of all kinds, ineluctable definitions of literature and philosophy – these Lyotard and his confrères regard suspiciously. By extension, normative notions of the literary critic disinterestedly and extrinsically writing about literature or the philosopher pellucidly and oracularly writing about ideas or values are thought by postmodernists to be specious; their manoeuvres have come to be thought of as falsely profound ploys. Criticism, Lyotard says, "has the pretension to situate itself in a pure exteriority":

---

[1] Jean-François Lyotard, "Réponse à la question: qu'est-ce que le postmoderne?," *Critique: Revue générale des publications françaises et étrangères*, No. 419 (April 1982), p. 366. Trans. and quoted by Georges Van Den Abbeele, "Up Against the *Wall*: The Stage of Judgement," *diacritics: a review of contemporary criticism*, 14, No. 3 (1984), 96-97.

The odds are that it will remain in the service of the apparatus it is out to get. It is a property of this apparatus that it indefinitely redoubles itself and includes within itself the exteriority from which it is criticized. A nasty trick is played upon the majority of religious, philosophical, political and esthetic "oppositions" in the course of Western history each time that they invoke an Other of the discourses and practices they are attacking. They do not attest to the fact that this Other is by construction implicated in the organization of the opposing field, and that they are thus themselves part, if not of its theater, at least of its theatricality even before they have commenced the dismantling of the representation. There is therefore a renewing of the imposture.[1]

Here Lyotard enunciates the dilemma of the expert who attempts to criticize from a privileged position, one external to the scene upon which s/he is commentating. No such disinterested vantage point exists, according to Lyotard. There is no space remote from discourse, from history, which allows one the omniscient perspective. Moreover, the expert, regardless of his or her stance towards the discourse, affirms its validity as a discourse merely by contributing to the field.

For Lyotard, as for French feminist theorists such as Luce Irigaray and Hélène Cixous, who seek to deny a patriarchal or phallocentric discourse, to write and therefore reconstitute oneself and one's culture differently involves something far more difficult than mere renunciation of the "Other," the antagonist. As Larysa Mykyta queries, seeking to present a feminist credo, how can one act and/or write given that " . . . both seeing and speech are masculine,"[2] bound up in the dominant culture? Her tentative answer is that on the practical level what is demanded is "the assumption of phallic positions,

---

[1] Jean-François Lyotard, *Rudiments païens: genre dissertatif* (Paris: UGE, collection 10/18, 1977), pp. 34-35. Trans. and quoted by Georges Van Den Abbeele, p. 93.

[2] Larysa Mykyta, "Lacan, Literature and the Look: Woman in the Eye of Psychoanalysis," *Substance*, No. 39 (1983), p. 56.

of power and authority, of equal rights and equal opportunities, of women speaking and writing, of women speaking and writing about women. But this alone is not enough for it does not question or disturb the *structures* of power and repression."[1] Direct, confrontational activity, though necessary, is not thought to be revolutionary enough, binding one, as Lyotard foresaw, into the dialectic which legitimizes that which is to be extirpated. Consequently, the medium of language and reflexive writing strategies need to be battled rather than deployed. Hortatory and polemical attitudes give way to a more arcane undoing of rhetorical devices. As Foucault's examinations of various institutions (penal, medical, sexual) have made abundantly clear, power is not necessarily exercised directly and can be eliminated simplistically.

Lyotard's own answer regarding how to elude theoretical traps, to permit heterogeneity rather than hierarchy to prevail is, he writes, parody: "The destruction of theory can only take place through parody; in no way does it consist in *criticizing* theory, since criticism is itself a theoretical *Moment* from which the destruction of theory cannot be expected. To destroy theory is to make one or some pseudo-theories; the theoretical crime is to fabricate theory-fictions."[2] Certainly, a reading of post-modern fiction reveals the dominance of parody: Donald Barthelme's *Snow White*, again to name one of a plethora of parodic works, is a compendium of parodies, some focusing on easy targets, some complex enough to reflect back on Barthelme's novel in process. In all cases, though, there is the recognition that no stable position exists from which a critique of society and art can be launched. Thus the postmodern writer, be he Derrida or Pynchon, must proceed by neither acceding unconsciously to nor attacking heavyhandedly some entrenched stance. In a review of some of Lyotard's works, Timothy Murray presents the altered approach required of the postmodern critic in the following manner: "When the critical imperative to understand, to translate, to systematize is

---

[1] Mykyta, p. 56.

[2] Lyotard, *Rudiments païens*, p. 29. Trans. and quoted by Georges Van Den Abbeele, p. 91.

dis-placed in the realm of the figural, the most familiar remaining product of philosophy is the empty gesture of the *demande* [demand/desire/question] undercut by its own plastic obliqueness, by its postmodern condition."[1] That condition pierces the plenitude of the subject, be s/he critic or philosopher, and her/his explanations, commentaries, or summaries, as well as her/his traditional responsibilities.

Lyotard's postmodernism eschews what Cecile Lindsay, another reviewer of Lyotard's work, calls "those grand explicating metanarratives"[2] which include such staples of cultural ordering as the notion of cause and effect, speculative philosophy and Marxism, not to mention traditional fiction. Piety characterizes the orthodox response to the metanarratives (criticism so often being reverential and hagiographical) and in its place Lyotard substitutes "pagan instructions": experimentation, paradoxes, the self-application of doubt. Lindsay quotes Lyotard as disdaining the purposive, purposeful attainment of wisdom: "Confidence . . . maintains activity and thought in the belief that the true is the most important thing . . . . This is the persistence of Platonism today: the prejudice that there is a reality to know."[3] An entire group of theorists whom Richard Rorty calls "abnormal" – Derrida, Foucault, and Lacan – would be foremost in such a group as would Thomas Kuhn and Paul Feyerabend, philosophers of science for whom scientific theories are paradigms, tenable hypotheses, not absolute truths, as well as the postmodern writers of fiction whose iconoclastic methods I have delineated briefly here and at greater length in *A Tale of Two Countries*, an earlier book of mine – seeks to have that prejudice attenuated. Lyotard's pagan is a tactician whose games with their constantly shifting rules undermine the content and forms by which a stylized reality has become known. In a polemical conclusion to *Instructions païennes*, Lyotard urges eradication of the taxonomies through which knowledge has been transmitted and the experts who have codified those

---

[1] Timothy Murray, "What's Happening?" *diacritics*, 14, No. 3 (1984), 104.

[2] Cecile Lindsay, "Experiments in Postmodern Dialogue," *diacritics*, 14, No. 3 (1984), 52.

[3] Lindsay, p. 55.

groupings. He demands that experimental, postmodern thinkers work to reveal ideology as itself fiction, fabrication, narrative:

> Destroy narrative monopolies.... Strip the narrator of the privilege he grants himself. Valorize the equally important power that lies on the side of reception as well as the power of execution, the narrated side. Struggle instead for the inclusion of metanarratives, theories, and doctrines, especially political ones, in the set of narratives. May the intelligentsia have as its function not to tell the truth and save the world, but to will the capacity to enact, hear, and tell stories.[1]

Writing fiction has always, of course, had story-telling as one of its major elements. As E.L. Doctorow has pointed out in an essay entitled "False Documents," such an admission confirms the prejudices of a public used to validating unthinkingly the false documents of sociologists, psychologists, historians, etc. as true ones. Rather than confirming the soundness of the parameters framing discourses regarded as authentic and the insights generated by traditional and flourishing modes of inquiry, those with a postmodern sensibility try to destabilize even the most respected intellectual systems. Thus, for Lyotard as for Doctorow, art which reveals its extravagant falseness, which flaunts and eschews its hallowed conventions, art, in short, which is experimental, is recognized as a more vital enterprise than the seemingly more august practices of social scientists or traditional humanists (not to mention traditional novelists). Lyotard writes:

> Can a given genre, for example the theater, tolerate "cruelty" the way in which Artaud understands it? Can painting tolerate Malevitch's "supreme"? Can literature tolerate Butor's "book-object" or Gertrude Stein's "paragraph"? By breaking down the boundaries of

---

[1] Jean-François Lyotard, *Instructions païennes* (Paris: Galilée, 1977), pp. 86-87. Trans. and quoted by Cecile Lindsay, p. 59.

different genres, these works engender their confusion.... In this way is constituted a universe of experimentation with forms, which can be termed satirical in the sense that the genres are mixed together (satura), and that the program for each is to saturate the tolerable.[1]

With the miscegenation of genres comes the reduction of those genres' ontological status. Similarly, such experimentation dilutes the power of academic discourses which have been kept remote from one another and which have been hierarchized.

Although many professors of literature are reluctant to see deconstructed the hierarchies about art they have created (consequently the tenuous and peripheral inclusion of postmodern literature and the avant-garde into the mainstream of literature programs), art is seen by Lyotard and other postmodern theorists as the most malleable medium for experimentation and, concomitantly, for subversion. Because the conventions of art are catalogued and classified primarily by English professors and literary critics, and because a great many conventions of artistic orthodoxy in periods other than the contemporary one were overthrown, art is regarded as a suitable instrument for unearthing the conventionality in the truth claims of other structures, other discourses. Lyotard's emphasis in many of his works, most notably *The Postmodern Condition*, is clearly the destabilization of the notion of a repository of knowledge contributed to and administered by experts in various fields. Postmodernism, in contradistinction to other sensibilities, demands first a recognition of the diverse and elusive nature of language games and second, a related awareness regarding the seemingly disinterested social-cultural-political fields which are studied in universities. Whereas previous estimations of the quest for knowledge included an acceptance of the holistic concept of that pursuit, regardless whether a different interpretation of it was being offered in different historical periods, postmodern theories define a fissi-

---

[1] Jean-François Lyotard, *Politiques de la philosophie* (Paris: Grasset, 1976), p. 125. Trans. and quoted by Cecile Lindsay, p. 61.

parous condition in which knowledge cannot be contained, in which language's possibilities are limitless – " . . . an infinite, or in any case an indefinite, number of phrases remains possible at each instant."[1]

In one of Barthelme's unorthodox short stories, someone asks "Is the novel dead?" only to be met with the query "Is the bicycle dead?"[2] Certainly the traditional novel, though practised still, for the most part doggedly and mechanically, on occasion with panache and incisiveness, is dead; nonetheless, there is a different kind of novel being written as there is a different kind of bicycle being produced. This latter novel fosters a post-modern awareness that many wish to extirpate (let us ignore for a moment the different intellectual demands it makes on a reader as well as the threat it offers to those teachers who teach Jane Austen and Charles Dickens as the avatars of novel-writing) because it threatens their ideological comforts. In *Father and Son* the Victorian Edmund Gosse wrote a poignant reminiscence about his father, whose inability to accept evolutionary notions precipitated desperate and tenuous intellectual manoeuvres, not to mention a breakdown. In our own era hysterical responses to postmodernism such as Gerald Graff's *Literature Against Itself*, Charles Newman's *The Post-Modern Aura*, and Mary McCarthy's *Ideas and the Novel*, which inveigh against the unique current orientation to fiction-writing and critical theory as cataclysmically demolishing cherished ways, are produced to bulwark an enervated climate of opinion and to resist the postmodernist formulations which I have skeletally demarcated. There is, however, in the practice of so many artists and thinkers a heterogeneous set of experiments, aperçus, and methodologies which collectively articulate a contemporary sensibility that retrogressive tracts can fulminate against but cannot abrogate.

The split from a more established framework can be presented in many ways, but one which contains a sharp differentiation between contrary ways of interpreting the world is

---

[1] Jean-François Lyotard, "Interview," *diacritics*, 14, No. 3 (1984), 17.

[2] Donald Barthelme, "The Explanation," *City Life* (New York: Farrar, Straus & Giroux, 1970), p. 70.

imaged in the difference between "readerly" and "writerly" that Roland Barthes has outlined in *S/Z*. The "readerly" or classical text contains an articulate message from a discrete source; the "writerly" or experimental text cannot be read in any one way and does not have one controlled and controllable meaning. That a revamped notion of art, self, and world challenges the form and content of a university, appropriating Barthe's concepts to examine the academy, many postmodern thinkers connected in one way or another with that venerable institution have acknowledged. For Lyotard, " . . . in the discourse of the University, as in those of the capitalist or totalitarian states, certain narratives are elevated over others because they are seen as containing the truth of the others or as constituting merchandise for turning a profit."[1] This readerly, rather than a writerly, university is what Lyotard rejects and what consensus appears to understand as the idea of a university.

Two more antithetical definitions of the university than those offered by Lyotard and by J.M. Cameron in *On the Idea of a University* could not be found. In an interview for the special issue of *diacritics: a review of contemporary criticism* devoted to his works and ideas, Lyotard is asked the following question:

> In *La condition postmoderne*, you speak of postmodernity as "ringing the deathknell of the era of the professor" . . . . [W]hat do you feel to be the pedagogical responsibilities of those of us still engaged in "classical" university teaching? What alternatives can you propose to the great Enlightenment narrative of education as emancipation?[2]

Much of Lyotard's answer devolves around resistance, "resistance against the academic genres of discourse to the extent that they forbid the reception of the 'is it happening that ... ?,' against the great narratives themselves, ... resistance against

---

[1] Lindsay, p. 61.

[2] Lyotard, "Interview," p. 18.

every object of thought which is given to be grasped through some obvious delimitation, method, or end."[1] Also, what Lyotard calls "good criteria" are not available to the postmodern teacher the way that "good forms" are useless to the postmodern artist. The organizing principles of traditional university teaching are regarded as sceptically as the great narratives which have been too institutionalized, ingested too fully. The threat of the subsumption and smoothing of academic practices, moves which mix "what dominant thought needs to separate in order to maintain its sober dominance,"[2] is noxiously ever-present to Lyotard. Theory always threatens to extend its grasp and to present itself as seamless, impeccable discourse.

To anyone who has read Foucault's treatises on the rise of institutions which control and regulate beyond their boundaries, and to those who respond positively to the aleatory art of, among others, Pynchon and Fowles, such a perception of the university is congruent with a sense of the traditional institution as homogeneous and autocratic. For all its nostrums about academic freedoms and tenure, the university has been felt by many to operate hierarchically and dictatorially to validate disciplines or subjects, methodologies (tests and the like), and administrative superstructures (which usually include a long-term president and various minions). To be sure there was a countervailing libertarian tendency in the late 1960s which produced some stunning confrontations at the University of California, Berkeley, and at Columbia, to name but two schools, and some utopian enclaves such as Kresge College at Santa Cruz and the College for Human Services in New York, both of which are discussed at length in *The Perpetual Dream* by Gerald Grant and David Riesman. For the most part such anarchistic moments and milieus have disappeared. To anyone with the slightest dissident temperament who has spent an extended period of time in a university environment, nonetheless, such responses are probably necessary and intuitive options in the face of a bureaucratic, professional, authoritarian context that greets one in the guise of freedom of course choices, research

---

[1] Lyotard, "Interview," p. 18.

[2] Lindsay, p. 61.

options, as well as parliamentary department, and university-wide debates. The trappings of deference (to professors as authorities, to the knowledge of which those professors are repositories and founts), gentility, and, above all, standards, still permeate academe; indeed, given the aging of the professoriat they have, if anything, been augmented.

Amidst what has come to be known as the crisis in the university (cf. Peter Scott's *The Crisis of the University*, J.M. Cameron's "The Crisis of the University," and William Cain's *The Crisis in Criticism*), which is a response to what has followed the counter-cultural thrust of the libertarians, namely the bankrupting of most universities, there has been a plethora of investigations as to how to re-establish a cogent direction for universities. Cameron's *On the Idea of a University* is not an atypical example of the kind of conservative revaluation that serves to affirm again the idea of a university as culled from Cardinal Newman's often cited *The Idea of a University*. (For a fusty and over-praised American version, see Allan Bloom's *The Closing of the American Mind*.) Such redefinitions are remote from Lyotard's or Derrida's disruptive postmodern directions and, when and if university administrators and government policy makers think about programs in the humanities, are usually the nostrums heeded (after clichés about pragmatism and job training have been uttered). Cameron's book, which comprises lectures delivered on the occasion of the 150th birthday of the University of Toronto and the 125th birthday of St. Michael's College, with its sure handling of a neutral medium, language, and its tone redolent of logic and reason, contrasts markedly with the products of postmodernism, not only Lyotard's and Derrida's but also Gregory L. Ulmer's (whose *Applied Grammatology* is a sustained and relentless application of Derrida's theories to education), especially insofar as what is taken for granted is concerned.

On the Idea of a University reads, despite its concern for the institution, like many serene and nostalgic works which invoke the halcyon days when the university more closely approximated, in the minds of those who think of themselves as the cognoscenti, the ideal university that Newman defined. This is not to say that Cameron is not angry or anxious, but those emotions are directed at many of the changes that took place in the early and middle 1970s. Cameron's book was published in 1978 and seems as remote from a postmodernist engagement with university theory and practice as a traditional novel, say one written by a current practitioner such as Robertson Davies, is from Barthelme's *Snow White* or Cortázar's *Hopscotch*. The comparison is not inapposite, for Davies found much to dislike in the academic experiments and upheavals of recent years. Diluting the impact of examinations and increasing the array of course selections cause distaste to Cameron as he commends something anathema to avant-garde theorists, the "natural" characteristics of a liberal education. He approbatively synthesizes the program and principles of William Cobbett's utopia:

> ... the grouping is "natural," not a chance coming together of persons related only externally (this is the principle that an educational enterprise is quasi-familial or collegiate); the impulse to learn comes from the desire to imitate models, in this case the father, offered by older people and from a natural curiosity prompted by the way they live; the father – the teacher – has a "natural" authority .... [1]

The conventional and sentimental picture of the ennobled and ennobling intellectual community is here encapsulated. Its good intentions, of course, are manifest, embodying the virtues of a liberal education enunciated by Newman for whom such studies are not utilitarian but intrinsically "good"; in addition, the studies delineated by Cameron "produce a special kind of man, that great exemplar of civility, the gentleman."[2] To many ears (needless to say predominantly masculine and classically educated) such a credo still sounds like the ideal definition. Never mind (if you can) its sexism, never mind its assumptions about a natural pursuit, about models freed of historical determination, about the possibility of a disinterested gentleman.

---

[1] J.M. Cameron, *On the Idea of a University* (Toronto: Univ. of Toronto Press, 1978), p. 12.

[2] Cameron, p. 13.

Here you have an expression of a desire for the civilized university peopled by founts of wisdom. That such a construct can be posited to an intellectual audience betrays the nostalgia for good forms which Lyotard for one has railed against. In his remarks Cameron yokes "Black studies, Gay studies, Women's studies, The Occult, Yoga, Astrology, UFO studies" and labels them "doubtful."[1] Such a patriarchal, paternalistic (one might add even less polite words such as obtuse and bigoted) summary not only betrays its prejudices but also leaves unquestioned the parameters of Newman's university. The traditional university is a stable edifice needing no intellectual shoring, so Cameron assumes; it is not historical invention marked by the period's idiosyncracies and blind spots. If English, History, Philosophy, and Classical languages (let us capitalize them to recognize the inflationary status accorded them) were the cornerstones of education until hippies and/or Ronald Reagan (let us juxtapose the two as constituting the perceived enemy) maligned them, then they deserve reinstitution or reaffirmation; aberrations – anything lacking a lineage or pedigree – deserve to be rebuffed.

The ideal university to J.M. Cameron, as it is to Northrop Frye whose "educated imagination" is fashioned in that environment, is corporeal, an enduring entity which must occasionally battle iconoclastic or avant-garde intruders. If change is acceded to, it is only insofar as T.S. Eliot (along with Newman and Matthew Arnold, avatars of the classical order) incorporates it in "Tradition and the Individual Talent." For Eliot tradition, too, is tangible – an aggregate body which is modified slightly when a meritorious individual talent is added. There is no chance of any occurrence such as the introduction of thought or a thinker which casts doubt on or devalues the collective enterprise. There is not even a modicum of engagement with or interest in the trenchantly rhetorical question asked by Ulmer: "What might be the ideal of an educated person proposed by a poststructuralism that puts in question the very notion of truth, in which the claims of truth to objectivity and neutrality are

---

[1] Cameron, p. 46.

exposed as effects of an apparatus of power?"[1]

It is no wonder that given his obtuseness Cameron sounds complacent compared to the postmodernists. His values are never tested rigorously; the gentleman who is a product of civility is never assessed ironically as artifice, a product of a specific social and historical context; the transparency of language as his medium is never doubted; positivism, logic, teleology are all tranquilly assimilated. Cameron concludes by stating: "About administration I say almost nothing directly. I think if we can get the work of the university right at the level of the classroom and the library we shall in fact make the university looser in its structure, having many different centres of power and interest. . . ."[2] First principles are safe and sacrosanct to Cameron. Thus, it is easy to see why his prose sounds laconic and assured in comparison with Lyotard's or Derrida's. The latter two take nothing for granted, neither their medium, nor the institution that antedates and in certain ways confines them, nor the products they themselves produce.

While a number of postmodern texts have found their way into North American curricula (Barthes, Derrida, and Pynchon are taught in many university departments), they are subsumed in an environment still saturated with a positivistic framework. Like Angel Clare in Thomas Hardy's *Tess of the d'Urbervilles* who proudly denounces his Christian dogma only to become ensnared by his Christian ethics, humanities teachers have in some cases presented a content-oriented postmodernism while leaving its implications for pedagogy and the humanities untouched; consequently, its impact is neutralized, appended to the dominant discourse which remains unscathed. While my pillorying of Cameron may seem to be a gratuitous, vituperative act, such is not the case. Simply put, Cameron's assumptions are themselves part of the problem. Moreover, the contemporary climate of opinion has been of little influence, unable to alter a stodgy institution. "Thank God, the sixties are over" uttered a colleague of mine only a few years ago, presumably

---

[1] Gregory L. Ulmer, *Applied Grammatology: Post(e)-Pedagogy from Jacques Derrida to Joseph Beuys* (Baltimore: Johns Hopkins Univ. Press, 1985), p. 168.

[2] Cameron, pp. 87-88.

because he could again go about his business of teaching what for him should naturally be taught. Far too little has been done to unnerve teachers and administrators of the humanities, to dismantle their taxonomies and dissipate their power. Whatever agitation has been produced has come externally from niggardly government funding agencies and the occasional truculent but impotent student.

Certainly, whenever bodies have been constituted to investigate and reinvigorate the teaching of the humanities they have produced flaccid, feckless recommendations as anachronistic as are Cameron's prescriptions. In 1978 the Rockefeller Foundation, for instance, sponsored a Commission on the Humanities which subsequently published *The Humanities in American Life*, a document which acknowledged the legitimacy of a liberal education only insofar as it produced literate citizens. Such is the state of American "culture." In the Province of Ontario the Bovey Commission, stocked by two senior university administrators and a "retired businessman," was no doubt congenitally incapable of calling into question the corporate-bureaucratic model of university governance. As seamlessly as does Cameron, the Commissioners introject themselves into the discourse of the university by accepting its hierarchies and its framework. To query the legitimacy of boards of governors, university presidents whose powers are built along the lines of senior executives of large businesses, and the whole phalanx of administrative appurtenances would not occur to men (*touché*) steeped in the model they are examining. Consequently, of course, they utter nostrums regarding the value of education and proceed to tax the least powerful group in the institution, the students. No doubt was cast on, for instance, the values of "professionalism." Illich (*Disabling Professions*) and Edgar Z. Friedenberg (*Deference to Authority*) might excoriate professionalism as one of mankind's most nefarious products, but a Commission saturated with professionalism, believing in careerism, in the inflation of the academic pursuit with its place in the upper echelons of the capitalist construct, would be and indeed was oblivious to the fact that "professionalism" *signifies*. That within the system its pernicious dimensions may be more of a problem than a perceived lowering of so-called academic standards or a multiplicity of arts programs in diverse universities the Commission was incapable of discovering. This is a consequence of an inquiry so sure of its scope that it does not question that scope.

All reification is a forgetting, according to Theodor Adorno; certainly, a narcotized group of officers responsible for dictating educational policy has ensued from such academic reification. Somnolence is one of the by-products of a self-confidence about the status of an institution and its purposes; this insight would probably shock Bovey et al., who would no doubt profess vigilance and acuity regarding the performance of their task. The political consequences of the maintenance of the status quo should be obvious from the above remarks. Perhaps the Bovey Commission, if it had been more attuned to postmodernism, would have recommended one way of minimizing professionalism: allowing *all* Ph.D.s to share in the salary pot, thereby increasing the number of incisive, committed people in the system. Sharing in a clerical model which would provide a far truer sense of collegiality than that fusty one presented by Cameron would have disastrous consequences for bourgeois-minded academics who would lose some of their power, lose some of their salaries, and be reduced in the eyes of doctors and lawyers, those other professionals who seem to control their destinies in a way which many academics desire. Such a set of arrangements, though, would create a body of intellectuals which does not have a stake in progress-through-the-ranks complacency and which might besiege somewhat impolitely the funding agencies which regulate universities' financial well-being. Instead of clamouring for a place in the hierarchy, young Ph.D.s would be freed to engage in a confrontation with extrinsic social agencies. This kind of scenario, I repeat, is, it is my guess, inconceivable for the Bovey Commissioners to imagine. Nonetheless, it would effect a far more dynamic revitalization than tinkering within the pre-existing system.

This is not to say that I am proposing utopian measures, some ideal university in place of Newman's and Cameron's. As Ulmer reminds one,

. . . all nonrepressive educational theories from Rousseau through Freud (to Reich and Marcuse) are finally utopian and are violent in their very illusion of being nonviolent. The conclusion that all such utopian pedagogies eventually self-destruct (being self-contradictory) would seem to be verified by the failure of the nonrepressive experiments in many universities in the wake of the student protest movement.[1]

Instead, my proposals are meant to counter the solidity the status quo always has, as well as to suggest alternative structures within which conflict and disruption can find new targets and activate new insights. Professionalism and seriousness need destabilizing, so entrenched are they in the academy. They are self-serving styles, not facilitating conduits, allowing professors untrammelled power and community status. Ulmer's chapter "The Scene of Teaching" in *Applied Grammatology* contains many suggestions and ploys which augment the intellectual enema I wish to provide – one which evacuates from, rather than contributes to, an exponential build-up of knowledge which is not intrinsically valuable, but which has been generated by structures left in place far too long. Ulmer writes, "The postmodernizing of pedagogy is based on the recognition that knowledge in and of the humanities is precisely a knowledge of enframing, of media and *mise en scène* understood not as a representation of something else but as itself a mode of action in the cultural world."[2] The result of such a pedagogy would not institute more advanced (not to mention simply more) content entering a student from an authoritative source, but rather the creation of a "meta-student," one engaged actively in the creation of categories and the recognition of the ironies and omissions inherent in those categories.

What Ulmer champions is an education built on Werner Heisenberg's principle of indeterminacy – the awareness of the observer's role – in lieu of the classical model in which a static world is captured and presented without distortion; if, indeed,

---

[1] Ulmer, p. 169.

[2] Ulmer, p. 183.

our notion of the physical world has shifted, why should not our academies' attempts to represent it (or as a deconstructionist might write, re-present it)? Earlier in the twentieth century, William Carlos Williams railed against the construction of traditional verse, calling it outdated amidst more relativistic objects created by men and women; Williams, of course, was seminal in the revision of the conventions of poetry. One could ask, echoing him, why the university and its taxonomies should remain stagnant, impervious to an altered concept of world. Ulmer's ambitious project, densely argued and heavily dependent on Derrida's essays, seeks a revamped university which would reflect a postmodern consciousness. Instead of a neutral institution autonomously distanced from a political-social morass, a sacred enclave producing educated "gentlemen," Ulmer's model has as its starting point awareness that " . . . education is a device of power and control whose chief purpose is to reproduce the dominant values of society and to legitimize the authority of the state . . . . [I]deals of universalism and nationalism are now perceived as problems rather than as objectives."[1] Again, Ulmer, echoing Derrida, warns that the libertarian rejection of this power arrangement and legitimization depends on a misconception that " . . . the system has an 'outside,' "[2] an error similar to Cameron's conservative hypothesis. There have, it is true, been institutions or collectives created with avant-garde precepts more in the foreground than in established universities – one thinks of the Frankfurt School or Lacan's École Freudienne or the institute Derrida has proposed to open; however, Ulmer's – and my – main focus is the re-evaluation and destabilization of more enduring universities and their humanities programs.

"*The classroom as a place of invention rather than of reproduction*"[3] : this maxim develops from the Derridean perception that a pedagogic deed of transmitting data through the conduits of teacher and language is a contaminated one. In *Dissemination* and *Reproduction*, among other works, Derrida stresses that

---

[1] Ulmer, p. 169.

[2] Ulmer, p. 169.

[3] Ulmer, pp. 163-64.

delusion awaits any criticism which is thought of as a transparent act of translation; moreover, teaching itself is probably the thing most emphatically conveyed to the students by the professor. Thus, an educational reform group in which Derrida participated whose acronym GREPH stands for "groupe de recherches sur l'enseignement philosophique" produced an anthology which encapsulated what Ulmer calls the "new imperative" of replacing "the purely intellectual, distanced, neutralized transmission of information (the ideological image of pedagogical communication) with a paradoxical technique of affective knowledge."[1] He then turns to Bernard Pautrat, one of the contributors to GREPH, for the following quotation which captures the shift in emphasis:

> It will be necessary one day to begin to use fully these margins of the professor's discourse, the place, the size of the audience, the sexual division, the disposition of the bodies, all that without which there would not even be a philosophic discourse. It is necessary to change scenes, if one thinks that the scene, by the complexity of its entreaties in which it plays, short of and beyond the gesture alone, the voice alone, is even to signify elsewhere, otherwise than in the intellect alone, the truth to be communicated. *A good scene is always worth more than a long discourse* in order to reveal the reality of exploitation, the reality of sexual difference, because it tends to take from behind the intellectual defenses, the very ones which entrust truth to the intellect alone without practice and without force.[2]

Other adaptations of postmodernism to teaching can be found in the *Yale French Studies* special issue number 63, *The Pedagogical Imperative: Teaching as Literary Genre*, devoted to contemporary pedagogy. Both Shoshana Felman and Angela S. Moger articulate positions that have been elucidated above. The

---

[1] Ulmer, p. 173.

[2] Ulmer, p. 173.

latter writes, "The pedagogical stance is a pretext that there is something substantive to be deciphered and appropriated."[1] To "experts" or "professionals" such debunking constitutes a threat to their power, the hegemony which is the fiduciary currency they use to fortify their self-esteem in a culture which would not heed them otherwise. In the first essay of the *YFS* issue Paul de Man acknowledges that the strong resistance among many members of English departments (few administrators are even aware of the incendiary potential of recondite critical texts) occurs as a result of the threat to the discipline's autonomy and ontological sureness. If it were merely a different methodology, easily adapted to the explication of texts the way, say, Northrop Frye's writings sustain an archetypal mode of inquiry into literature, discomfort would be minimal. Helen Gardner's sane disquisition on the way English studies were initially formulated in Britain contains an instructive tale for those who cannot accede to any alteration in practice or theory. Gardner reveals that in the constitution of the English program the study of Anglo-Saxon and Philology was incorporated not because they were intrinsically related to an English program but because of "the notion of English as a 'soft option,' a subject which exists for the benefit of the weaker brethren, and particularly the weaker sisters . . . ."[2] So much for the definition of the discipline as inviolable and true. Gardner goes on to say, "I suspect that the same uneasiness in [the] face of the charge of 'softness' is one motive behind the various attempts in our own day to professionalize English literature . . . ."[3]

Academic business must, according to the corporate-bureaucratic model, be a growth industry, one which generates some *thing*. Borges's paean to leisure as being central to the style of the literati and Proust's cultivation of the majestic beauty of something wonderfully unnecessary – these are not calculated to appeal to people in business and government

---

[1] Angela S. Moger, "That Obscure Object of Narrative," *Yale French Studies*, No. 63 (1982), p. 135.

[2] Helen Gardner, "The Academic Study of English Literature," *Critical Quarterly*, 1 (1959), p. 106.

[3] Gardner, p. 106.

leaders whose own scope, I am sure, would also not be enlarged to admit the play of the postmodernist. Such frivolity is not consonant with professionalism, with the production of data, never mind whether other readings of *A Tale of Two Cities* or sociological and psychological forays into human conduct are merely by-products of the form and content of their disciplines. A visit to the Learned Societies to hear scholarly papers would most assuredly (and perhaps injuriously) convince one of the gravity with which academic research proceeds. Papers are delivered without any sense that the context has shifted from the pages of a scholarly journal to a public forum; turgidity inadequately describes the atmosphere. There is a torpor on the institutional level as well. Ironically, a university whose primary activity is the examination of its own assumptions and parameters seems far too self-reflexive, far too paralytic to those who don't dismiss it outright as a threat to their livelihoods. The fusty demand in literature for the study primarily of dead authors and an aversion to the avant-garde are easy to understand given a typical notion of the university. Dead authors and fully defined periods are commodities, easily packaged into the early years, the middle years, and the late years. If they lend themselves to multiple interpretations, they nevertheless do not challenge the status of the investigators.

The arbitrary and seemingly inviolable power of university hierarchies, both administrative and pedagogic, will simply not do. Certainly, a good many feminist theorists find in the continuation of the status quo an insupportable phallocentric situation. Such writers as Julia Kristeva, Hélène Cixous, and Luce Irigaray, postmodernist in their scepticism regarding unitary meanings, experiment with the forms of fiction and essay writing, among others, in a radical way akin to Derrida's. Their desire is to break the hold of a patriarchal authoritarian institution's dispensation of knowledge. As Elaine Marks and Isabelle de Courtivron, the editors of an anthology entitled *New French Feminisms*, affirm, the goal of women's writing is to decentre phallic authority. They write in a footnote in their introduction:

The verb *jouir* ("to enjoy, to experience sexual pleasure") and the substantive *la jouissance* ("sexual pleasure, bliss, rapture") occur frequently in the texts of the new French feminisms. We have constantly used the English words "sexual pleasure" in our translations. This pleasure, when attributed to a woman, is considered to be of a different order from the pleasure that is represented within the male libidinal economy often described in terms of the capitalist gain and profit motive. Women's *jouissance* carries with it the notion of fluidity, diffusion, duration. It is a kind of potlatch in the world of orgasms, a giving, expending, dispensing of pleasure without concern about ends or closure.[1]

This description contains parallels with the definition of the postmodern university I have been presenting. Here, feminism is not merely a matter of equal right, however important that may be on a pragmatic level; feminism, rather, is a radicalism. Control, teleology, concentrated power – these are minimized according to Marks's and de Courtivron's redefinition. To appoint a conservative university president who happens to be a woman instead of a conservative university president who happens to be a man does not violate the old order. Interestingly, in her 1984 address as president of the Modern Language Association, Carolyn G. Heilbrun cites the excitement generated for women as a result of the nomination by the Democratic party of Geraldine Ferraro as its vice-presidential candidate. Well, Angela Davis, a far more articulate, far more untrammelled and intellectual woman, was a vice-presidential nominee before Geraldine Ferraro, and is a far more fitting role model (if one looks for such things) if feminism is to realize its incendiary potential; however, Davis, of course, was the candidate of the Communist party, far too marginal an entity (despite a *pro forma* obeisance to Derrida's *Margins of Philosophy*) than American academia is ready for. Not that the feminists antholo-

---

[1] Elaine Marks and Isabelle de Courtivron, eds., "Introduction III: Contexts of the New French Feminisms," *New French Feminisms: An Anthology* (New York: Schocken, 1981), pp. 36-37.

gized in *New French Feminisms* (especially Irigaray whose *Speculum of the Other Women* and *This Sex Which Is Not One* display a deconstructionist temperament as insistent as Derrida's) spend a great deal of time enunciating political credos. Direct action is taken for granted in some cases. In others it is regarded as too facile – the equivalent of the libertarians' attempts to step outside social systems to create a utopian institution. One manifesto by a radical feminist group defends opting out of a contribution to the history of feminism, "a history of Feminism which thus, here, is compelled to acknowledge on its reverse side the other-counter side of the old order."[1] Strategies akin to those of experimental fiction-writers or postmodern theorists are thought to be more valuable than transparent, content-oriented measures.

Hélène Cixous's "The Laugh of the Medusa" contains an ecstatic paean to the liberation of women's bodies by postmodernist writing. While it is difficult to imagine the university, as glacial as most institutions are in its response to innovation, being transformed, postmodernist modes supplanting authoritarian ones, it is easy enough to show any inquisitive student that an emerging unique sensibility demands unique expression. Because the gap between a protean humanity and the rigidified humanities is so great and because innovative artists and thinkers have already dismantled many orthodoxies, revealing the gap, that task will continue to be more greatly facilitated. – I am catching myself right now because the last sentence ends with the kind of uplift which is a staple of traditional literary criticism. I should let you know that I have been banned for life from one of the University of Waterloo pubs and am in no way to be trusted to determine models or directions for you or anyone else.

---

[1] Marks and de Courtivron, p. 32.

Michel Foucault's Touchstones

"Every man is his own rotisserie." – Grace Paley

"It takes toot to tango." – Thomas McGuane

"If orgasm is the pit of the fruit, then lyricism is its flesh." – John Hawkes

"In every act of pedagogy there is an element of pederasty." – Jane Gallop

"Good taste is acquired censorship." – Gaston Bachelard

"Negative Clank: He'd sell a rat's asshole to a blindman for a wedding ring." – Richard Brautigan

"Imagination rules the world, shithead." – Robert Coover

"O gimme some o' that acne, à-la-mode,
Eat so much – that Ah, jes' ex-plode!
Say there budd*ih* you can chow all nite, on
Toe-jam tarts 'n' Diarrhea Dee-lite . . . . " – Thomas Pynchon

These don't sound like Matthew Arnold's touchstones, you say, Shakespeare's, Milton's, and Dante's orotund moral nuggets blasphemed by the connection? Perhaps there is too little "truth and seriousness" for you? "The superior character of truth and seriousness, in the matter and substance of the best poetry," Arnold preaches in "The Study of Poetry," "is inseparable from the superiority of diction and movement marking its style and manner."[1] The yoking of truth and gravity, as well as of lofty content and lofty form, though it has metamorphosed some-what through the flux of twentieth century critical styles, has

[1] Matthew Arnold, "The Study of Poetry," in *Prose of the Victorian Period*, ed. William E. Buckler (Boston: Houghton Mifflin, 1958), p. 509.

43

not been fundamentally rejected. Gravity's rainbow, in other words, still attempts to contain (not to mention subjugate) *Gravity's Rainbow*. The Arnoldian hangover extends beyond sobriety and high seriousness: to canonization and hagiography, to elevation of the antiquarian, to uplift, to hierarchization, to rigidification.

Although Terry Eagleton (*Literary Theory: An Introduction*), Ihab Hassan (*Paracriticisms*), Edward Said (*The World, the Text, and the Critic*), and Frank Lentricchia (*Criticism and Social Change*) are among a number of recent combative critics who have in various ways confronted the reification of literature by the academy and its officers, it is Michel Foucault who has most adroitly skewered the institutions and their keepers, as well as the elaborately self-serving ways they have generated and codified humanity and its accoutrements: literature, knowledge, sickness, power, etc. For Foucault, the machinery with which we produce meanings, data, categories, insights and the like, with which we authenticate and explain experience, may just be a Rube Goldberg machine – its systems conferring quests, truths, and problems which are self-validating. Orthodox analyses and orthodox modes of investigation have become too reflexive, too "natural," too authoritative. The professions and bureaucracies that they have spawned have by now generated such momentum that their first premises are secured, never challenged. Their boundaries and margins are rarely the focus of those who operate in them and even study them. The overwhelming quantity of research into literature, for example, is rarely thought to be institutionally generated and consequently self-reflexive, even tautological. Moreover, in epistemological terms, the methodology of the professions (and the professors) validates metaphors of depth, continuity, origin, and totality, the metaphorical dimensions of which are masked. This methodology also centripetally authenticates the subject as researcher and *his/her* subject, the research. In such a positivistic atmosphere is most academic research produced.

Foucault's texts are recondite because they are congruent with his notion that culture cannot be read transparently, that professions and disciplines cannot understand, synthesize, or interpret culture positivistically via language. As Hayden White writes in an article dealing with Foucault, all language is catachresis,[1] or misuse. Like Vladimir Nabokov with his use of a fictional foreward in *Lolita*, like John Barth who insults "the reader! You, dogged, uninsultable, print-oriented bastard ...," [2] Foucault teases and dodges readers who appropriate his works for traditional ways of reading and understanding. Like Derrida and Jacques Lacan, Foucault writes prose which is replete with puns and other ludic exercises to deny readers scientific, totalizing overviews of man. Foucault wishes to avoid his work being subjected to the interpretive strategies so ingrained in readers. "I would not like it for a book to give itself the status of a text that could be handled reductively as a result either of pedagogy or criticism."[3]

If postmodern fiction, or what has been called metafiction, challenges precepts of mimesis, teleology, and referentiality, then so, too, does the poststructuralist writing of Foucault and Derrida. As enunciated by Foucault, four notions "(signification, originality, unity, creation) have ... dominated the traditional history of ideas; by general agreement one sought the point of creation, the unity of a work, of a period or a theme, one looked also for the mark of individual originality and the infinite wealth of hidden meanings."[4] Both for postmodernists and poststructuralists, one cannot resolve the game of the world, enmeshed as one is in that anarchic game, in language and in milieu. Words do not simply and directly interpret the world (even if there were an interpretable world). There is no recourse to originary meaning or originary presence in order to prove something or discover a truth. "Discourse must be

---

[1] Hayden White, "Michel Foucault," in *Structuralism and Since: From Lévi-Strauss to Derrida*, ed. John Sturrock (Oxford: Oxford Univ. Press, 1979), pp. 81-115.

[2] John Barth, *Lost in the Funhouse: Fiction for Print, Tape, Live Voice* (New York: Bantam, 1969), p. 123.

[3] Michel Foucault, *Histoire de la folie à l'âge classique* (Paris: Gallimard, 1977), p. 8. Excerpt trans. by Edward Said in *The World, the Text, and the Critic* (Cambridge, Mass.: Harvard Univ. Press, 1983), p. 215.

[4] Michel Foucault, "The Discourse on Language," in *The Archaeology of Knowledge*, trans. A.M. Sheridan Smith (New York: Pantheon, 1972), p. 230.

treated as a discontinuous activity . . . . "[1] As for Thomas Kuhn (*The Structure of Scientific Revolutions*) and Paul Feyerabend (*Against Method: Outline of an Anarchistic Theory of Knowledge*), as well as for two of Foucault's mentors, Gaston Bachelard and Georges Canguilhem, scientific forays and intellectual pursuits of all kinds produce systems of classification, not representations of reality. Or as Coover articulates it, "all conceptualizing . . . [is] a kind of fiction-making."[2] More dangerously, the conceptualizing becomes systematized, reified, and rigidified.

His apposite metaphor, the Borges story which he cites at the beginning of *The Order of Things*, reveals Foucault's fascination with our catachrestic structures, with what is thinkable, sayable, possible, with what "bears the stamp of our age and our geography."[3] It discloses further the limitations on the statements one makes, the categories one deploys – the stylized taxonomic enterprise that Borges and all the writers of metafiction parody. Foucault seeks to scrutinize the stylized formation of discourse which dictates, in a broad sense, what is said, what is validly said, and, most importantly, who says it. "I am supposing," writes Foucault, "that in every society the production of discourse is at once controlled, selected, organised and redistributed according to a certain number of procedures, whose role is to avert its powers and its dangers, to cope with chance events, to evade its ponderous, awesome materiality."[4] Criticism should be seen, as one of Foucault's acolytes, Said, writes,

inhabiting a much contested cultural space, in which what has counted in the continuity and transmission of knowledge has been the signifier, as an event that has left lasting traces upon the human subject. Once we take

---

[1] Foucault, "The Discourse on Language," p. 229.

[2] Christopher Bigsby, "Interview with Robert Coover," in *The Radical Imagination and the Liberal Tradition: Interviews with English and American Novelists*, eds. Heide Ziegler and Christopher Bigsby (London: Junction, 1982), p. 82.

[3] Michel Foucault, *The Order of Things: An Archaeology of the Human Sciences* (New York: Vintage, 1973), p. xv.

[4] Foucault, "The Discourse on Language," p. 216.

that view, then literature as an isolated paddock in the broad cultural field disappears, and with it too the harmless rhetoric of self-delighting humanism.[1]

The ontological security of "literature," "genres," and "literary criticism" disappears in such a formulation. Criticism becomes a more subversive, less approbative act. The stable body of works, an Arnoldian touchstone, operated on assuredly to produce a stable body of insights – metaphysical, psychological, sociological – is revealed more as a product of structures and systems than as an intrinsically coherent entity.

Foucault and those he has influenced (White, Said, and Eagleton, for instance) mainly emphasize the way literature is defined and compartmentalized, the discipline that has grown up around it, its systems and vocabularies, its inclusions and exclusions as well as its university ambience. It is seen to be a highly stylized discourse designed to keep professors of English literature in control of a reified field. It allows them to become productive professionals (and, extrapolating further, "solid" citizens) with a domain to police and regulate. The genteel image, the Arnoldian touchstones (alias the classics, the cultural stature) – these are assimilated into the university with *its* compartments and professional stratification in such a way that literary criticism appears to be naturally enmeshed and comfortably ensconced in an institution. Tenure, a lifetime supply of "Norton Critical Anthologies," a modicum of money, and an abundance of "kulchur" are the ancillary accoutrements of the profession.

Traditionally, literature is a solid edifice, a club with fixed and selective membership; traditionally, literary criticism is hagiography, the passing of a hallowed tradition, a clean, well-lighted place (and these days, also, one with a fixed and selective membership which precludes over-crowding or even displacement). The grooming and maintaining of a national literature are redolent of such a framing. The creation and inflation of cultural idols, the entitlement to a place in the

---

[1] Edward W. Said, *The World, The Text, and the Critic* (Cambridge, Mass.: Harvard Univ. Press, 1983), p. 225.

literary firmament, the development and enshrining of a well-defined national identity, corpus, literature – these are the staples and the *raison d'être* of, among others, "CanLit."

CanLit critics see their mission as one of constructing, rather than deconstructing. Moreover, their purpose is not merely disinterested uplift; it is the making of a tradition in the image of other national literatures. Finding a distinctive voice, freeing itself from colonial fetters, enshrining its greats and proclaiming their greatness – these are the stereotyped dimensions of empire building, literary variety. In addition, the consignment of this task to literary critics gives them control of the discourse as well as a messianic calling. (No mere aestheticism or dilettantism here.) It also permits them to canonize those who will take their place as "authors" in a "national" literature. Even more deleteriously, literary critics then seize on those "authors" whose detritus becomes talismanic, whose fugacious jottings (notes, drafts, letters, etc.) become iconic, valuable even. Such critics appear to an ironic reader to be akin to the doctors of Foucault's *Madness and Civilization*, the prison-keepers of his *Discipline and Punish: The Birth of the Prison*, and the sexologists of his *The History of Sexuality*. Nationalistic literary critics become, in short, professionals who authenticate a country's literary experience, validate themselves as curators of their country's literature, and invent and regulate the currency of art (Susan Musgrave's hankies and Hugh MacLennan's baseball cards gaining or losing value according to the whims of the market). The positivistic and acquisitive purpose of such an undertaking is masked as a natural one, the building of a national literature an unqualified good, a spontaneous thing (an "atoll"[1] according to Robertson Davies). What Northrop Frye describes as the "obvious and unquenchable desire of the Canadian cultural public to identify itself through its literature"[2] augments and buoys the whole process.

---

[1] Robertson Davies, "The Canada of Myth and Reality," in *Canadian Literature in the 70's*, eds. Paul Denham and Mary Jane Edwards (Toronto: Holt, Rinehart and Winston, 1980), p. 9.

[2] Northrop Frye, *The Bush Garden: Essays on the Canadian Imagination* (Toronto: House of Anansi, 1971), p. 216.

Looking into the Lacanian mirror, as it were, produces no ironic glimpses for the CanLit critics. They are sure of their propagandist roles. So, too, are British critics who see their national literature as the paradigm and *sine qua non* of criticism: a seamless body of British literature that is disseminated as the core of English speaking literatures, its periods and their characteristics recited formulaically in classrooms everywhere. Even the growing number of devotees of deconstruction have preferred to leave the framework of literary studies inviolable. Perhaps only Edward Said, whose *Orientalism* and *The World, the Text, and the Critic* focus on the arbitrary and even racist character of such a choice, has challenged the homogeneous, monolithic structure of English departments. Those who practise what Richard Rorty in *Philosophy and the Mirror of Nature* calls "abnormal" philosophy (Nietzsche and Derrida, for example), those who practise "abnormal" science (Kuhn and Feyerabend) or "abnormal" history (Foucault) – in other words, those who deconstruct their disciplines, attacking holistic and totalizing concepts – have not, despite deconstruction's current fashionable status, had a conspicuous impact on programs in departments of English literature.

For "abnormal" theorists and their maverick confrères, criticism is primarily an anarchistic, decentring activity that runs counter to the nurturing of national literatures as well as to disciplines generally with their attendant professional coteries. This kind of criticism is practised in a way which Foucault states is compatible with the role of a guerrilla fighter:

Writing only interests me to the extent that it unites itself to the reality of a combat, functioning as an instrument, a tactic, an illumination. I would like my books to be sorts of scalpels, Molotov cocktails, or minefields and have them carbonize after me in the

49

manner of fireworks .... I am a tool merchant, a
tactitian, an indicator of targets, a cartographer, a
draftsman, an armourer.[1]

To the question, "Can a literary intellectual ... do radical work
as a literary intellectual?,"[2] which preoccupies Lentricchia in
Criticism and Social Change, Foucault answers with a subversive,
incendiary criticism that does not congeal into an "oeuvre" or a
methodology. His revolutionary deconstruction is an immediate threat to staid institutions and programs, one of the most
vulnerable of which should be the discipline of English literature and its various epicene imitators. Interestingly and predictably, no nationalists have tried to shrug the colonial yoke in
such a deconstructive way. The process is probably too much of
an oxymoron. Builders have no use for boobytraps or minefields.

Literary history is another edifice destabilized by Fou-
caultian activity. His notion of genealogy decentres and dis-
rupts rather than contains and constructs. Roots, sources, and
lineage are not generated by genealogy. It is not a project which
creates "bodies of knowledge," "schools," "periods," and
"major figures," as well as classificatory systems of whatever
kind. "The purpose of history, guided by genealogy, is not to
discover the roots of our identity but to commit itself to its
dissipation."[3] Genealogy does not promote the kind of identity
that the search for an origin creates and verifies. Nor is it
teleological. History, literary or otherwise, does not proceed in a
linear, sequential manner.

Much postmodernist fiction has as its focus the rendering of
history as his/story. Coover's Richard Nixon, Joseph Heller's

---

[1] Jean-Louis Ezine [interviewer], "Sur la sellette: Michel Foucault," *Lies Nouvelles
Litteraires* 2477 (17 March 1975), p. 3. Excerpt trans. by Pamela Major-Poetzl in
Michel Foucault's Archeology of Western Culture: Toward a New Science of History
(Chapel Hill: Univ. of North Carolina Press, 1983), p. 43.

[2] Frank Lentricchia, *Criticism and Social Change* (Chicago: Univ. of Chicago Press,
1983), p. 2.

[3] Michel Foucault, *Language, Counter-Memory, Practice: Selected Essays and Interviews*, trans. Donald F. Bouchard and Sherry Simon, ed. Donald F. Bouchard
(Ithaca, N.Y.: Cornell Univ. Press, 1977), p. 162.

Henry Kissinger, Max Apple's Gerald Ford – these are just a few of the historical figures whose solidity as characters is undermined in metafiction. In "Robert Kennedy Saved From Drowning," Barthelme seeks to rescue Robert Kennedy from becoming an ossified symbol of the American identity. Written about the time of Kennedy's assassination, the story saves Kennedy from being reduced to martyr or symbol, or indeed to any other easy construct or character. Barthelme presents various views of Kennedy: the reminiscences of friends and former teachers, Kennedy's own comments, etc. These anecdotes are just the sort of stories that fill out the legends of public figures. They are also the stuff of most literary histories. But Barthelme does not let these snippets cohere into a fable; rather, he undercuts the myth-making with Kennedy's discussion of Marivaux.

The Marivaudian being is, according to Poulet a past-less, futureless man, born anew at every instant. The instants are points which organize themselves into a line, but what is important is the instant not the line. The Marivaudian being has in a sense no history. Nothing follows from what has been done before. He is constantly surprised. He cannot predict his own reaction to events. He is constantly *overtaken* by events. A condition of breathlessness and dazzlement surrounds him. In consequence he exists in a certain freshness which seems, if I may say so, very desirable.[1]

The Marivaudian being resists becoming the ponderous receptacle of traditional historians; he or she has no identity in the customary, the ontologically sure, sense of the word.[2]

Foucault's genealogy is a recalcitrant subject, resistant to origins, anti-teleological. "As it is wrong to search for descent in an uninterrupted continuity, we should avoid thinking of

---

[1] Donald Barthelme, "Robert Kennedy Saved From Drowning," in *Innovative Fiction*, eds. J. Klinkowitz and J. Somer (New York: Dell, 1972), p. 145.

[2] The above two paragraphs were contributed by Susan Gray.

emergence as the final term of an historical development . . . . "[1] Original meanings, final identities, reified subjects, practical research and researchers – to overthrow these things is to supplant a traditional with a postmodern perspective. As Ihab Hassan defines it, postmodernism is "playful, paratactical and deconstructionist."[2] Hassan celebrates the "abnormal" orientation which provides "evidence of disconfirmation," those "paratactical, paradoxical, paralogical narratives meant to open the structures of knowledge as of politics to language games, to imaginative reconstitutions that permit us either a new break-through or a change in the rules of the game itself."[3] John Hawkes's pithy maxim that the true enemies of the novel are plot, character, theme, and setting encapsulates the tendency towards experimentation taken by contemporary American writers of metafiction, French exponents of the *nouveau roman*, and South American fabulators in the manner of Borges.

While the contemporary novel has undergone a reorientation along the lines articulated above, most institutions, especially academic institutions and most disturbingly – and stodgily – the humanities, have balked at disintegration or dissolution of a postmodern nature. Ironically, but predictably, the controllers of those subjects with the shakiest claim to grounding, with perhaps the most anarchistic materials, resist most mightily any kind of structural tinkering. As Derrida reveals in his essays on the university ("Border Lines" and "The Principle of Reason: The University in the Eyes of its Pupils"), the assault on method, on framework, and on margins or boundaries contains an epistemological anarchism that threatens the professional's hegemony over "knowledge" (and concomitantly the professor's power over students).

---

[1] Foucault, *Language, Counter-Memory, Practice*, p. 148.

[2] Ihab Hassan, "Ideas of Cultural Change," in *Innovation/Renovation: New Perspectives on the Humanities*, eds. Ihab Hassan and Sally Hassan (Madison: Univ. of Wisconsin Press, 1983), p. 25.

[3] Hassan, p. 27.

The deconstruction of a pedagogical institution and all that it implies. What this institution cannot bear, is for anyone to tamper with [*toucher à*; also "touch," "change," "concern himself with"] language, meaning *both* the *national* language *and*, paradoxically, an ideal of translatability that neutralizes this national language. Nationalism and universalism. What this institution cannot bear is a transformation that leaves intact neither of these two complementary poles. It can bear more readily the most apparently revolutionary ideological sorts of "content," if only that content does not touch the borders of language [*la langue*] and of all the juridico-political contracts that it guarantees.[1]

Although the vocabulary of criticism has changed slightly, and although postmodernism does work its way into the diaspora of literary studies – as long as it does not contaminate august periods such as the Renaissance or the Romantic – it is still Greek to me. From "mimesis" to "aporia" is not as great a gap as might appear to some. It is certainly not as momentous as the move from "mimesis" to "horseshit."

The academy still tries to seize control of the vocabulary of criticism, whether it is appropriated from *Anatomy of Criticism* or *Of Grammatology*. Derrida astutely realizes this grasping on the part of the profession and so makes his terms arcane, interminable, even undefinable. Foucault, too, with the desire for his books to carbonize as fireworks, refused the academic canonizing of his vocabulary. Nonetheless, with workshops, seminars, indeed the entire paraphernalia of scholarship, academia insists on registering deconstruction and post-modernism as content, aberrant because of its contemporaneity but teachable. The academy employs translatability which produces a Berlitz equivalent of the language of post-modernism, one resembling the vocabulary of professionalism: simply a new language that graduate students must master in order to be admitted to the *same* country (and one, in these days

---

[1] Jacques Derrida, "Border Lines," in Harold Bloom et al., *Deconstruction and Criticism* (New York: Seabury, 1979), pp. 94-95.

of minimal employment opportunities, with stiff "wetback" laws, the equivalent of those recently debated in the United States Congress).

For Derrida and Foucault, anything that fosters method also fosters codification and professionalization, shoring up the institution and its hierarchizing apparatuses and vocabularies. In *La Vérité en peinture* Derrida writes:

> According to its very logic (deconstruction) would address not merely the internal constitution of philosophemes, in their semantic and formal aspects, but also what is generally but erroneously regarded as their external habitat, as the merely extrinsic conditions in which they are practised: the historical forms of their instruction, the social, economic or political structures of the pedagogical institution. It is because it touches upon such solid structures, such "material" institutions, and not merely upon discourses or signifying representations, that deconstruction is not merely analysis or "criticism." And to be pertinent, it must work, as strictly as possible in that place where the so-called internal operation of philosophy articulates itself in a necessary manner (i.e. internally *and* externally) with the institutional forms and conditions of teaching and learning. And it must carry this to the point where the concept of institution itself would be submitted to the same deconstructive treatment.[1]

What is demanded here is no less than a postmodern theory of the university generally and the humanities specifically. Derrida refuses to leave the form and boundaries of the institution sacrosanct and inviolable. Such an unsettling notion clashes with the antiquated and reified humanities as they are presently constituted in universities. It also threatens the narrow, arid terrain cautiously cultivated by specialists. Currently, periods

---

[1] Jacques Derrida, *La Vérité en peinture* (Paris: Flammarion, 1978), pp. 23-24. Excerpt trans. in Samuel Weber, "After Eight: Remarking Glyph," *Glyph: Johns Hopkins Textual Studies*, No. 8 (1981), pp. 236-37.

and authors are classified and hierarchized to the point where even a minor dismantling of the structure (much less of the "material" institution), say the supplanting of "Renaissance" by "postmodern" writers at the core of a literature program, would appear to be the grossest of tergiversations. Many faculty members would be rendered apoplectic.

Postmodern fiction, for instance, itself challenges the stability of institutions. Many, such as Barth's *Letters*, Barthelme's *Snow White*, or Coover's *The Universal Baseball Association, Inc.: J. Henry Waugh, Prop.*, contain direct attacks on "knowledge" and the way it is compartmentalized, disseminated, and assimilated; they note its stylization and arbitrariness. Foucault himself is predisposed to experimental art, to that art which collapses the accommodating bridge between word and world. He frequently cites Borges and Beckett, as well as writers such as the Marquis de Sade, Georges Bataille, and Raymond Roussel, whose works, he feels, tease orthodox extrapolations. In *This Is Not a Pipe*, his book on the painter René Magritte, his translator, James Harkness, reveals Magritte's bias which is congruent with Foucault's own: "The mystical, Platonic identification of words with the essences of things is what many of Magritte's canvases vigorously assault."[1] "Nonaffirmative Painting," the title of Chapter 6, can be extended as a pithy definition for all postmodern art. Throughout the book Foucault plays with Magritte's play with the discrepancy of signifier and signified. He reads Magritte's "pipe" paintings as, in part, undercutting the idea of the pedagogue as provider of meaning. "The essential point [for Foucault] is that resemblance and affirmation cannot be dissociated."[2] So he is drawn to those who do not affirm, to a painter such as Magritte who unsettles without moving fully into abstract art, whose unsettling of the boundary between image and legend, painting and title, words and things, is the stuff of his art. Magritte, Foucault writes, combats resemblance which "makes a unique assertion, always the same: This thing, that thing, yet another thing is something else [i.e., the object's

---

[1] Michel Foucault, *This Is Not a Pipe*, with illus. and letters by René Magritte, trans. and ed. by James Harkness (Berkeley: Univ. of California Press, 1982), p. 7.

[2] Foucault, *This Is Not a Pipe*, p. 34.

distinctiveness]."[1]

Postmodern fiction, anti-mimetic, anti-teleological, non-totalizing, and anti-referential as it is, confronts similar shibboleths. Nonetheless, the way it is usually taught and assimilated presents no threat to the ontologically secure institution whose structures it intrinsically taunts. Lyotard articulates the postmodernist manifesto in a manner akin to Derrida's, Foucault's, and Hassan's. The postmodern, for him,

> puts forward the unpresentable in presentation itself . . . that which searches for new presentations, not in order to enjoy them but in order to impart a stronger sense of the unpresentable. . . . [T]he text [a postmodern writer] writes, the work he produces are not in principle governed by preestablished rules, and they cannot be judged according to a determining judgment, by applying familiar categories to the text or to the work.[2]

Lyotard continues the assault of the "abnormal" theorists on the professional educators whose programs reek of positivism and inflexibility and whose institutions yield none of the destabilizing qualities of an ironic postmodern sensibility. Without such a revamped perspective no change to literary studies or to the humanities is possible. Despite Derrida's and Foucault's fertile intellectual experiments, despite their boundary crossing, their deliberately marginal discourse, their ludic exercises, their pyrotechnics will be (and have been) absorbed and centred by the institution.

Derrida has already warned that the discourses of Marxism and psychoanalysis, incipiently revolutionary and disruptive as they might have been, have been co-opted by the institution in such a way that they have been rendered homogeneous, indistinguishable from the discourse that dominates the university. Feminism, too, has for the most part been defused of its

---

[1] Foucault, *This Is Not a Pipe*, p. 46.

[2] Jean-François Lyotard, "Answering the Question: What is Postmodernism?" in *Innovation/Renovation: New Perspectives on the Humanities*, eds. Ihab Hassan and Sally Hassan (Madison: Univ. of Wisconsin Press, 1983), pp. 340-41.

radical potential. Certainly more women have been allowed into the academic enclave; however, their professionalism, their assumption of the "proper" academic discourse, assures the continuation of the institutional framework. The "cuntamination" that Gallop demands in *The Daughter's Seduction: Feminism and Psychoanalysis* has only minimally occurred. A different sexual ratio will preside over the same terrain, with the same rules and other such circumscriptions. Deconstruction has undergone similar absorption. Faculties of English and graduate students who aspire to those sublime realms have sought tirelessly to domesticate the works of Foucault et al. Despite the sometimes hysterical response to deconstruction by such conservatives as E.D. Hirsch, Jr., and M.H. Abrams, it remains a fiduciary currency, traded for a fixed thing – access to the university's hierarchy. The structure of English departments, their autonomy and inviolability, and their professional appurtenances (tenure, publish or perish, etc.) remain unshakable. Simply put, whenever the form of an institution stays impervious to or digests effortlessly new vocabularies and epistemologies, it has withstood any radical reorganization and guaranteed what Derrida has called its "juridico-political contracts."

Without the postmodern sensibility that denies the legitimacy of national literatures and of the taxonomies of the humanities, and that reviles the professionalism of education, the framework of intellectual pursuit is retained. It is by now an attenuated, inspissated structure. In literary studies specifically, the postmodern perspective must supplant the traditional view of literature as a stable body of works and authors with its inherent hierarchy (Shakespeare, the cynosure of the literati, Barthelme, say, a "lesser" figure). "Foucault's touchstones" are not meant merely to parody Arnold's. They challenge the premise of a genteel literature, a cultural attainment, as well as the cognoscenti who are supposedly its proper (in a few senses of that word) custodians and curators. Had he not died recently, perhaps Foucault's deconstructive focus might have one day turned on the academy; however, he had already used an apt title for such a study – *Discipline and Punish: The Birth of the Prison.*

LITERATURE

Gobble, Gobble, Gobble:
Critical Appetites

Casciato, Arthur D., and James L.W. West, III, eds. *Critical Essays on William Styron*. Boston: G.K. Hall, 1982.

Clerc, Charles, ed. *Approaches to 'Gravity's Rainbow'*. Columbus: Ohio State Univ. Press, 1983.

Kiernan, Robert F. *Gore Vidal*. New York: Frederick Ungar, 1982.

Molesworth, Charles. *Donald Barthelme's Fiction: The Ironist Saved From Drowning*. Columbia: Univ. of Missouri Press, 1982.

Porter, M. Gilbert. *The Art of Grit: Ken Kesey's Fiction*. Columbia: Univ. of Missouri Press, 1982.

"Literature" is omnivorous. Genteelly, with the proper fork, itself part of the inflexible recipe, it works its way relentlessly through the contemporary American world of words. "Authors" and "oeuvres" are its favourite comestibles. Obligingly, "Gore Vidal" is trussed. This is not, you understand, Gore Vidal, the one who several times taunted William F. Buckley, Jr., with the moniker "pro-crypto-Nazi" in a television debate, whereupon Buckley replied: "Now listen, you queer. Stop calling me a crypto-Nazi or I'll sock you in your goddamn face" (Kiernan, p. 7). This is "Gore Vidal," "author," creator of fifteen or so novels as well as numerous scripts, screenplays, and essays, whose output can be shown to reveal growth, consistency, coherence, and whose spat with Buckley would be placed in the category "anecdote."

Similarly, Ken Kesey is basted (not lambasted) and served up as "Ken Kesey," seamless author of three important works: *One Flew Over the Cuckoo's Nest*, *Sometimes a Great Notion*, and *Demon Box*. "Kesey's" career to date, containing as it does two "finished works of art" (M. Gilbert Porter's quotation marks taking over here) and one diffuse collection of baubles and deadends published recently, allows him to be understood as enmeshed in a crisis. Championing him, Porter writes the following in *The Art of Grit*: "Like Dante, Kesey seems to have found himself meandering in a murky wood away from the straight path, and, like Hemingway, he apparently feels he can liberate himself from his personal demons by writing them away . . ." (pp. 79-80). "Dante" and "Hemingway" are themselves authors who have been taken over by "literature." Unlike "Kesey," they are dead; also, unlike "Kesey" their status has been secured, their works accepted into the great tradition, their names hallowed. Their detritus – shopping lists (though it is hard to imagine Dante shopping; such is the hagiographical process), doodlings, notes to others – is, when found, cultivated and hoarded. The process of bronzing Kesey and his canon works this way, and Porter has begun the job (or rather, he continues it).

Foucault, in his essay "What Is an Author?" and elsewhere, assaults this notion of the author and his or her work of art with its indelible stamp as literature as well as its autonomy and iconographic place: " . . . what if, in a notebook filled with aphorisms, we find a reference, a reminder of an appointment, an address, or a laundry bill, should this be included in his works? Why not?"[1] Already, deconstruction, call it the Derridean microwave to keep the food motif alive, has served notice that it wishes to dismantle the heretofore inviolable tradition with its ineluctable subsections. Dante, Hemingway, Shakespeare, American Literature, Canadian Literature, novels, poems – the systems of inclusion and exclusions, the arbitrary categories and hierarchies, taxonomies of all kinds are what deconstruction has sought to expunge. The conservative goose, though, has not quite been cooked (even if Porter's yoking of Dante and Kesey causes the profession an acute case of indigestion, if not salmonella).

The point of these opening paragraphs is that contemporary literature, from the books under review, is clearly being prepared, offered, and digested in time-honoured ways, its authors

---

[1] Michel Foucault, "What Is an Author?" in *Language, Counter-Memory, Practice: Selected Essays and Interviews*, trans. Donald F. Bouchard and Sherry Simon, ed. Donald F. Bouchard (Ithaca, N.Y.: Cornell Univ. Press, 1977), pp. 118-19.

being inducted into "literature" by its academic hierophants. Vidal's voluminous dossier is brought into compartmentalized focus; Donald Barthelme is described as a maturing, evolving storywriter; Kesey is assessed as a writer of two (no doubt three now that *Demon Box* has been published) important books who is currently subjected to writer's block (no emetics yet being known to alleviate said condition). Such cookie-cutting sometimes seems silly. In *Edwin Mullhouse: The Life and Death of An American Writer, 1943-54, by Jeffrey Cartwright,* Steven Millhauser parodies biography. The intrepid Jeffrey takes over Edwin's adolescent leavings from his short life – eleven years – and divides the life and writings into the early years, the middle years, and the late years. Edwin is helpless to stop the assimilation of events and texts by "literature." The analogy with literary critics in America, Jeffrey Cartwrights most of them, is an apt one; they (we) dragoon the writings of the contemporary period into books on writers in which one faintly senses the muffled protests of those writers, Edwin Mullhouses most of them. Whether they like it or not, they acquire oeuvres, careers, problems.

Kesey is served most poorly by such a process. Simply put, it is because there are not enough ingredients. True, the life, LSD being the vital additive, is interesting and was captured wittily by Tom Wolfe in *The Electric Kool-Aid Acid Test.* As for an update, Porter tells us that Kesey is no longer the counter-cultural guru he once was; rather, he is "a serious artist" (p. 101). Approbatively told, this assertion only reminds me of Allen Ginsberg's plaint in "America" about *Time* magazine's seriousness: "It's always telling me about responsibility. Businessmen are serious. Movie producers are serious. Everybody's serious but me."[1] That was 1956 and now, my turn to be plaintive, Ginsberg, too, is serious. Kesey's seriousness, though, is more acute than Ginsberg's. In herculean fashion, Porter writes, he "labors over naming his characters to achieve an appropriate match between character and name" (p. 4). In *Sometimes a Great Notion* he has written "a novel whose every

---

[1] Allen Ginsberg, "America," in *Howl and Other Poems* (San Francisco: City Lights, 1956), p. 32.

notion is realized in rich, intrareferential concretions from beginning to end" (p. 78). Finally, in the pieces produced since the two novels, Kesey has struggled "heroically" to find and enounce meaning: "... underlying every movement is an intense quest for understanding, for direction, for form" (p. 80). In an uplifting conclusion (another staple of the critical cookbook), Porter reveals that Kesey is not only a serious moralist but also a "skilled writer of character and power with a chest full of purposeful tools" (p. 102). The ironic linking of Kesey with Nurse Ratched's powerful chest full of tools is, I am sure, unintentional. So, too, is the solecism on the book's back cover: "... underneath the face of the clown beats the heart of a dedicated, accomplished artist ...." Strange constellation of bodily features, indeed.

One Flew Over the Cuckoo's Nest is a powerful but simplistic novel in which nature is pitted against technology, outcasts against the middle class, Dionysus against Apollo. These polarities, as well as Chief Bromden's shift from "withdrawn schizophrenic to liberated man," have been charted many times. Because the novel is so direct, so polemical, it does not lend itself well to repeated synopses. Like paté, these paraphrases have become "pro forma." "The message of the novel" as revealed by Porter is the stock one; also, the mention of "the poetic first-person point-of-view" no longer surprises. Similarly, the elements of *Sometimes a Great Notion*, though not as obvious as those in Kesey's first novel, have had their articulation. Inclusion of a discussion of *Demon Box*'s salmagundi only reiterates the limitations of the "author" approach to Kesey. The man wrote one novel which forcefully confronts monolithic America and its straitjacketing effects. This need not force him to assume the mantle of professional writer. To produce a book about "Kesey," the one who undertakes such a project seems to feel obliged to develop sequence and causality in the author's work, to engage all the published material, to present the voice that supposedly unified the words. Part of the difficulty may be that Porter is writing for a series, Literary Frontiers Editions, which has dealt with such diverse contemporary writers as Gabriel García Márquez, Tom Stoppard, R.P. Blackmur, and Robert Graves; the demands of the series, perhaps, coerce the author into inflating Kesey into "Kesey." The former, really, was interesting enough, a fauvist who, like Vidal and Truman Capote (and Ginsberg, too), creates a more engaging self than art.

If Kesey is a fauvist, Barthelme is a metafictionist (this *in medias res*-ipe should also include the traditionalists, William Styron representing them, as the third of the three styles of writing prevalent in contemporary American fiction). His sense that artifice rather than nature saturates humanity's social, intellectual, and emotional attributes, that character in and out of fiction is a construct and that realistic fiction is stylized and ideological marks him as a metafictionist. In a masterful story called "Critique de la Vie Quotidienne" Barthelme captures the clichéd quality of modern living. He presents a *de rigueur* couple whose *de rigueur* house and family lead to a *de rigueur* divorce: " 'There has been a sixty percent increase in single-person households in the last ten years, according to the Bureau of the Census,' I told her. 'Perhaps we are part of a trend.' "[1] After the divorce the child attends a nursery school operated according to Piagetian principles. Everything, in short, is done stylishly. For Barthelme, similarly, everything people do is stylish; nothing is natural.

Charles Molesworth's book on Barthelme's fiction also appears in the Literary Frontiers Editions series; although it is only eighty-nine pages long, it is a good deal more stylish than Porter's book. *Donald Barthelme's Fiction* is quite tenaciously argued; Molesworth does not merely survey the fiction, choosing instead to unearth the roles parody and irony, especially, play in Barthelme's work and by extension in metafiction as a whole. To this end the book is insightful and successful. Alan Wilde's review of *Donald Barthelme's Fiction* in *Salmagundi* (No. 60) even makes the point that Molesworth abandons the concept of "oeuvre," the metaphor of organicism. To an extent he does. He refuses, for instance, to discuss the novels, *Snow White* and *The Dead Father*, referring to them as extensions of Barthelme's experiments with the short story form. He also deals with the stories only insofar as they impinge on the

---

[1] Donald Barthelme, *Sadness* (New York: Pocket Books, 1980), p. 20.

problems of form and language. In the "Conclusion," though, Molesworth restively tries to confer on Barthelme some place in the grand literary scheme of things. He asks whether Barthelme, like James Joyce, has "a belief in the transcendent, universalizing power of art" (p. 82). Moreover, he queries whether Barthelme has a meliorist's view of civilization, whether he is alert to "the evil of banality" and whether he has "a sense of the problem of thnic destiny" (p. 83). Because Molesworth feels he must answer "no" to each question, because he feels Barthelme lacks "a central philosophical, historical, or metaphysical given" (p. 83), he consigns him to a rank beneath that of a major writer. Barthelme's immense parodic skills, however, vitiate even this judgement. In the questionnaire which is placed at the end of "Part One" of *Snow White*, Barthelme asks the following: "Holding in mind all works of fiction since the War, in all languages, how would you rate the present work, on a scale of one to ten, so far? (Please circle your answer) 1 2 3 4 5 6 7 8 9 10."[1]

Recognition of the gap between signifier and signified is evidently not a sufficiently weighty perception to raise Barthelme's stock in Molesworth's estimation. He concludes *Donald Barthelme's Fiction* on an expansive and uplifting note that does not agree with, for instance, the titles with which Barthelme ends *Snow White*. Molesworth writes:

Barthelme is saved from drowning in a world of fragments by his ironic manipulation of them. And he is saved from drowning in his own irony by a commitment to those fragments as the saving reality. He does this by sacrificing any consistently inward feeling of a final truth. But he never lets us forget how the absence of such a truth feels. And from *that*, we can almost see the truth for ourselves. (p. 89)

One can imagine this passage in Barthelme's hands: "Author saved from drowning! Credits ironic manipulation for keeping him afloat in sea of fragments."

---

[1] Donald Barthelme, *Snow White* (New York: Atheneum, 1972), p. 83.

Final truths are, of course, anathema to the metafictionists whose writings sometimes have a palinodic or palindromic structure when they don't deny teleology by more disruptive means. The absence of a final truth feels neither better nor worse than the presence of such an entity, except that for the postmodernist the latter is a fiction to which they cannot accede. Molesworth seems to be regretful that Barthelme's refusal to accept a vision or to take a stance prohibits him from occupying an ennobled place in the annals of "literature"; he is reduced, in Molesworth's estimation, to finger food (hors d'oeuvres?). This summation betrays Molesworth's longing for hierarchies and meanings more than it denotes Barthelme's limitations. In his search for some *thing* in Barthelme's works, Molesworth even persists in over-valuing the collage and the fragment which Barthelme has chided other critics for seizing on. All tend to elevate the maxim, fragments are the only form I trust, into a dictum and a nostrum. All want to provide the uplifting overview, that essential ingredient in the critic's art. Perorations, wedding artist's vision to world, appear regularly, even in such would-be deconstructionist works as Said's *The World, the Text, and the Critic*. Some of the essays in *Approaches to 'Gravity's Rainbow'* are also prone to the grandiose closing statement turning Pynchon's labyrinthine novel into a heartfelt message or *cri du coeur*.

Nonetheless, Molesworth's book contains some incisive commentary on Barthelme, especially by comparison with, say, Jack Hicks's *In the Singer's Temple*, Paul Bruss's *Victims: Textual Strategies in Recent American Fiction*, or other pieces on Barthelme that treat his plot and characters far too realistically. Metafiction often befuddles and teases academic critics, sometimes pre-empting their scholarly remarks (as in *Snow White*), other times parodying their totalizing efforts (as in Barth's *Chimera*). It mocks the systems that critics build around it and undercuts the overviews they proffer. Regarding the prevalence of parody in metafiction generally and Barthelme's fiction specifically, Molesworth explores the subtlety of the genre that many hostile readers of metafiction miss when they berate the postmodernists for their abundant use of parody. For Molesworth, Barthelme deploys parody not as heavyhanded mockery or burlesque; rather, "parody, as Barthelme uses it, is a mocking irony . . . " (p. 45) which does not clearly reduce or belittle the parodied object:

> . . . there is seldom a single clearly parodied structure or content against which a 'straight' or serious counterpart is being set . . . . The story becomes a field of free-floating parody, where no anchoring content or style serves as the central vehicle of intention against which the other structures are judged or interpreted. (p. 46)

The ironic voice which itself can be ironized, in Molesworth's phrasing, is what he has to contend with in presenting a sense of Barthelme's fiction. Such constant undercutting is not easily amenable to the taxonomic enterprise in which Molesworth persists. He divides the stories into five groups: total aleatory structure, the surreal place, the counterpointed plot, the extended conceit, parodies of narrative structure. Why not a fiction index, placing the stories on an extended scale (0% to 100%) which would see "Robert Kennedy Saved From Drowning" and "The Ford-Carter Debate" linked because of their use of "real" personages? In addition, Molesworth makes too much of the short story form. Barth, Coover, Gass, and Pynchon, as well as Barthelme, write novels as well as short stories; moreover, the boundary is not a clearly defined one. Coover's *Spanking the Maid* is called a novel despite containing under one hundred pages. Fiction, not the short story, novel, or novella, is the vital medium with which the metafictionist contends.

Molesworth's problem, finally, is that he does not partake of the metafictive temperament. Despite an astute mind, he appears to be comfortable with more traditional works of fiction than Barthelme's. He sounds like the John Gardner of *On Moral Fiction* when he writes that " . . . if we come to stories more for a reflection of how we live now, or even more seriously as a criticism of life, Barthelme's playful use of fragments will strike us as irresponsible and ludicrous" (p. 31). Like Porter and *Time*, Molesworth wants seriousness. Barthelme's insights into the artificial, stylized ways people live, his sense of the cliché-rid-den nature of language (Snow White utters, "O I wish there were some words in the world that were not the words I always hear!"),[1] even more acutely, his recognition that all language is catachresis or misuse – these are not good enough for Molesworth, who wants serious thematics or a recognition that Barthelme is only a minor master. Neither Barthelme, nor Coover, nor Pynchon needs such an apologist. Recently, Eagleton in *Literary Theory: An Introduction* and *William Shakespeare* (both books deliberately titled inappropriately) recognized that Shakespeare's place at the top of the literary heap is part ideology and part cliché. Only ideology and cliché keep metafiction's texts and practitioners minor.

Robert F. Kiernan's *Gore Vidal* is a more placidly written book in qualitative, if not quantitative, terms. Kiernan is sure of Vidal's stature: "The great charm of Vidal's writing is its auctorial audacity .... It is a bravura performance withal, and in a sense Vidal is less a storyteller than a performer .... The Vidalian persona, *con brio*, is the ultimate achievement of Vidal's arts" (p. 144). Gore Vidal, in short, has failed to become what he so desperately wanted to be: "Gore Vidal," author and novelist, inductee into "great literature." Instead, what Ihab Hassan wrote of Gass applies to Vidal on a much more modest scale: he "can write sentences, by the hundreds, that would tempt Torquemada to forgive for each word a heretic at the stake."[2] Without Gass's metaphysical erudition and wit, Vidal, nonetheless, writes with panache and elan about the American milieu. Essays such as those on the Reagans, the university novel, or "the hacks of academe" display Vidal's own wit as well as his trenchant nastiness: "Ronnie" Reagan he refers to not as a president but rather an indolent cue card reader; "Unlike the United States, Italy has both an educational system (good or bad is immaterial) and a common culture, both good and bad."[3] In another instance, he sniped at Leslie Fiedler, taking him to task for slighting William Dean Howells (about

---

[1] Barthelme, *Snow White*, p. 6.

[2] Ihab Hassan, "Wars of Desire, Politics of the Word," *Salmagundi*, No. 55 (1982), p. 118.

[3] Gore Vidal, "On Italo Calvino," *The New York Review of Books*, 21 Nov. 1985, p. 3.

whom Vidal wrote a fine essay in *The New York Review of Books*, which provides Vidal his best forum, an intellectual but unacademic one):

> ... there is something wrong with a critical bias that insists upon, above all else, "dream and nightmare, fantasy and fear" but then when faced with the genuine article ... starts to back off, nervously, lighting candles to The Family and all the other life-enhancing if unsmiling aspects of American life that do *not* cause AIDS or social unrest.[1]

The essay on Howells provides an opportunity to see Vidal at his most judicious, valuing Howells's novels for their non-hermetic, non-bookish focuses. Their worldliness is what Vidal probably aspires to in his own fiction.

Unfortunately, that fiction is too mechanistic, undermining Vidal's desires for authorship. It is Kiernan's chore, the quantitative dimension of his book, to present an overview of Vidal's voluminous output. *Gore Vidal* is part of the "Modern Literature Series" which now numbers approximately one hundred books on writers ranging from Agnon to Zuckmayer. Slight books, their emphases devolve on the explication of individual works that make up an author's canon. Kiernan obligingly discusses and offers synopses of novels (from *Williwaw* to *Creation* to *Kalki*) which no one reads anymore. He even touts *Myra Breckenridge* and its sequel, *Myron*, as "probably the most important novels about Hollywood since Nathanael West's *The Day of the Locust*" (p. 94). He refuses, though, to indulge in hagiography, even expressing disappointment in the essays which, he writes, "are more interesting for their quips, their anecdotes, and their satirical exaggerations than for the spine of essayistic logic" (pp. 116-17).

If Gore Vidal has required little assistance in becoming a personality, William Styron has needed little aid in gaining recognition as an "author." His first novel was labelled by

---

[1] Gore Vidal, " 'The Peculiar American Stamp,' " *The New York Review of Books*, 27 Oct. 1983, p. 52.

many critics as fraught with promise and was regarded as "serious"; his later work has come to grips with momentous topics such as race, morality, and the Holocaust. His vocation sanctified by the critical community with varying degrees of endorsement, he has not shirked from dealing with the most meaningful problems confronting humanity, equivalent to a chef's attempting to perfect gâteau St. Honore or Peking duck. The William Styron papers are already nestled in the Library of Congress; letters and other memorabilia are safely ensconced in the library at Duke University; *The Confessions of Nat Turner* won the Pulitzer Prize in 1968; Larzer Ziff's encomium to *Sophie's Choice* concludes by stating that Styron asserts "art's power and thus art's right to break in upon even sacred silence" (p. 244).

Critical Essays on William Styron, itself part of a series, Critical Essays on American Literature, both directly and obliquely seeks to confirm this image of Styron. Its format, consistent with others in the series and unlike that of the books discussed above, offers reviews of and essays on his major works by diverse critics; that the books comprise the "author" is the premise here. The advantage of such an approach is the diversity of viewpoints provided; the disadvantage is the repetition of plot summaries. Because Styron is what G.A.M. Janssens calls "the author of the grand theme" (p. 269), most of the commentators presented in this book are respectful, even awed. Harvey Breit thinks of Styron as Dostoevskian; John Gardner calls him "the savior of all America!" (p. 247). Perhaps it is my tepid response to gâteau St. Honore, but the controversy surrounding *The Confessions of Nat Turner* and *Sophie's Choice* (blacks vilifying Styron for tampering with history's Nat Turner, Jews for creating Sophie Zawistowska as the non-Jewish heroine of the novel or for sensationalizing the Holocaust experience) outstrips the impact of those books. While images of the exploitation of black slaves and the desecration of the death camps are heightened by the novels' scenes, the scenes themselves are only adjuncts to the historical facts. Greater novels need no antecedents or *prima facie* material to make their impact.

For those who wish to gain a better sense of Styron's work, though, *Critical Essays on William Styron* includes some worthwhile pieces. Anthony Winner's article, "Adjustment, Tragic Humanism and Italy: Styron's *Set This House on Fire*," has a wonderful preamble on the use of Italy as a metaphor in literature, before it engages the novel itself. Mike Thelwell's and Eugene D. Genovese's debate on the merits of *The Confessions of Nat Turner*, as well as on the proper appropriation of historical facts in fiction, is also interesting. So, too, is the section devoted to Styron's reception in France where his notoriety is said to be great and his links with the *nouveau roman* are acknowledged. Melvin J. Friedman's essay on the latter topic points to one of the gaps in the casebook. It is the only one to examine the form of Styron's fiction, the editors content to write only, "Unlike many of his contemporaries, Styron has remained loyal to the traditional novel as a literary form" (p. 8).

Thomas Pynchon betrayed no such loyalty in writing *Gravity's Rainbow*, a novel which, the dust-jacket of *Approaches to 'Gravity's Rainbow'* proclaims, "has seemed almost to defy an imposition of critical order." Thankfully, this reviewer shouts, relieved to reveal his anarchist-cum-deconstructionist bias. Amidst all the cookbooks, culinary and academic, there is no recipe here, no recipe for "life." Everyone's bent for the blessed rage to order is taunted and thwarted. In the lexicon of *The Crying of Lot 49* and the marvellous *Gravity's Rainbow*, Maxwell's Demon can be thought but not actualized. Violating the second law of thermodynamics, the sorting and organizing Demon orders its molecular universe; critics try to do the same thing, placing relevant sections of novels in coherent explanations to reveal what Pynchon calls "pulsing stelliferous Meaning." Such activity, though, according to Pynchon, is doomed to failure. Presenting a compartmentalized, interpreted *Gravity's Rainbow* is akin to presenting a compartmentalized, interpreted universe – a futile or falsifying enterprise. Both book and world contain a myriad of clues, both coax one into accepting systems, but both withhold their centres and sources, "the direct, epileptic Word," as Pynchon names it in *The Crying of Lot 49*. Nonetheless, there lurks that universe of *Gravity's Rainbow*, seven hundred and sixty pages in the Viking edition.

The world and words of *Gravity's Rainbow* are dispersed. Each of the critics whose articles are gathered in *Approaches to 'Gravity's Rainbow'* recognizes the novel's condition; however, some do succumb to the temptation to play Maxwell's Demon, to sort and order the dense novel. "Like other sorts of paranoia, it is nothing less than the onset, the leading edge, of the discovery that *everything is connected*, everything in the Creation, a secondary illumination – not yet blindingly One, but at least connected . . . . "[1] Many of the paranoiac critics make fine efforts. The best two essays are the first two: "War as Background in *Gravity's Rainbow*," by Khachig Tololyan and "Science and Technology," by Alan J. Friedman. The first provides an understanding of Pynchon's non-dualistic, non-dialectical thinking. Tololyan understands that, like Foucault's books which he cites, *Gravity's Rainbow* does not contain a simplistic war/peace, powerful/powerless dichotomy. He also has a great deal of insight into the sources Pynchon used for his understanding of World War II. Friedman's essay elucidates the sophisticated scientific theories that one finds in *Gravity's Rainbow* (and that make it one of the few *science* fiction novels). To those nurtured by "literature," it is shocking to have to contend with quantum physics, information theory, et al. Not the least of the pleasures of *Gravity's Rainbow* is that it challenges the limits of one's diet. Journals such as *Perspectives in Biology and Medicine* and *Journal of the Institute of Actuaries* are brought into the "literary" ambit. Thankfully, again, *Gravity's Rainbow* is more voracious even than "literature." What is more, it is not genteel; no table manners are needed.

Oh gimme some o' that acne, à-la-mode,
Eat so much – that Ah, jes' ex-plode!
Say there budd*ih* you can chow all nite, on
Toe-jam tarts 'n' Diarrhea Dee-lite . . . .[2]

---

[1] Thomas Pynchon, *Gravity's Rainbow* (New York: Viking, 1973), p. 703.

[2] Pynchon, p. 717.

POSTSCRIPT: A review of Jay Cantor's *The Death of Che Guevara* in *The New York Review of Books* confirms my contention that the concept of "oeuvre" is a preoccupation of many critics. Robert Towers writes: "It will be interesting to see what direction this gifted writer will take now . . . ."[1] Cantor's novel is a "first novel," his vocation confirmed. Were he once to make a good bouillabaisse, would *Gourmet* magazine follow his career ever after?

---

[1] Robert Towers, "El Novel," *The New York Review of Books*, 8 Dec. 1983, p. 40.

The Importance of Being Earnest: Literary Critics in America

By a poet I do not mean one who writes poems, but a terrorist or provocateur who *never* writes . . .

– Arrabal

Douglas, George H. *Edmund Wilson's America*. Lexington: Univ. Press of Kentucky, 1983.

Fishbein, Leslie. *Rebels in Bohemia: The Radicals of 'The Masses,' 1911-1917*. Chapel Hill: Univ. of North Carolina Press, 1982.

Jay, Gregory S. *T.S. Eliot and the Poetics of Literary History*. Baton Rouge: Louisiana State Univ. Press, 1983.

Said, Edward. *The World, the Text, and the Critic*. Cambridge, Mass.: Harvard Univ. Press, 1983.

Stern, Frederick C. *F.O. Matthiessen: Christian Socialist as Critic*. Chapel Hill: Univ. of North Carolina Press, 1981.

Every so often literary critics, living as they do in a culture that regards their pursuit as a frippery, as something remote from the so-called real world, get the jitters. Either to themselves, their students, or their readers they launch an *apologia pro vita sua*. Although drawn to what Proust called the majestic beauty of something wonderfully unnecessary, an ideal critics usually savour, they find themselves at some point on the defensive, their vocation appearing as elitist, arcane, or jaded beside the hefty doings of their seemingly more committed colleagues and non-university professional neighbours. *The World, the Text, and the Critic* is Edward Said's *cri du coeur*, but it is only one of many recent confrontations of critics with their roles.

The enunciation of one's credo occurs most frequently in a period of upheaval, one in which unestablished theories appear to be supplanting more traditional ones. One has only to think, for instance, of the apocalyptic titles of Geoffrey Hartman's recent work – *The Fate of Reading, Criticism in the Wilderness*, and

75

Saving the Text – to realize that critics do not feel their operations are solely hermetic or scholastic enterprises. Augmented by such collections as *The Pedagogical Imperative* and Ihab and Sally Hassan's collection *Innovation/Renovation*, which push literary theory towards a redefinition of the university, and books such as Lentricchia's *Criticism and Social Change* and John Fekete's *The Critical Twilight*, as well as portions of Vincent B. Leitch's *Deconstructive Criticism*, which broaden the arena to include society at large, literary criticism claims for itself a role far from the feckless pastime with which the discipline has, in common parlance, been saddled.

Such an upheaval is surely one of the more salutary contributions of deconstruction. With the displacement of Frye, New Criticism, and T.S. Eliot (finally) from the inner sanctum has come a critical mode that has altered the ordering of world, text, and critic. Especially since criticism has flourished in the academy, there has been no shortage of justifications for the critic's mediating role between text and world; however, the perplexing status of text as a part of, yet apart from, the world has not heretofore had the usurpation proffered by Hartman, among others: " . . . literary commentary may cross the line and become as demanding as literature: it is an unpredictable or unstable genre that cannot be subordinated, a priori, to its referential or commentating function."[1] Criticism has rarely been thought of as unpredictable or unstable; on the contrary, the scientific framework offered by Frye or the close, disinterested reading tendered by the New Critics stressed just the opposite. Criticism has always been regarded as a conservative entity, one which has formed and articulated the genre "literature," that is, until deconstruction has put "literature," "author," "oeuvre," "masterpiece," and "tradition," among many others, *sous rature*. As Hartman maintains, "Only one thing is certain. There is no putting the djinn back into the bottle."[2]

Such erosion of critical and, concomitantly, cultural staples

---

[1] Geoffrey Hartman, *Criticism in the Wilderness: The Study of Literature Today* (New Haven: Yale Univ. Press, 1980), p. 201.

[2] Geoffrey Hartman, *Saving the Text: Literature/Derrida/Philosophy* (Baltimore: Johns Hopkins Univ. Press, 1981), p. 21.

should perhaps be recognized as something different from some of the late 1960s and early 1970s American formulations which had, as their *raison d'être*, the reduction of the critic's status and putative power to form and dictate taste. As refreshing as was Louis Kampf's diatribe against the profession, in his year-end presidential address to the Modern Language Association memorably entitled " 'It's Alright, Ma (I'm Only Bleeding)': Literature and Language in the Academy," deconstruction's challenge to the pre-existing arrangement of world, text, and critic is different in that it does not advocate unmediated intercourse between world and text. Although the critic as "expert" is diminished by deconstruction, nothing quite as uncomplex as Jerry Farber's dictum about professors and literary critics being jail-keepers and slave masters (gathered in Farber's collection entitled *The Student As Nigger* which, of course, contains most memorably the essay of the same name) is presented.

Certainly, deconstruction is (or can be) just as unsettling and anti-authoritarian as the pronouncements of Farber, Kampf, and other counter-cultural antagonists of the Vietnam era; however, the role of the critic, though it no longer has its hegemonic status intact, does not altogether disappear. Nor is it regarded as an unmitigatedly uplifting pursuit. Kampf, bless him, yearned directly and holistically for "unity of ideological purpose and economic necessity, of leisure and the way I earned my daily bread .... I felt confident that performing my task as a literary man would improve my own life, that of my students, and humanity in general."[1] To effect such a utopian milieu, narrowness and professionalism would be proscribed; moreover, extrapolating from Kampf's remarks, the hierarchies of the institution would have to be dismantled. Selective hiring practices and tenure would have to give way to collegiality and the clerical model. Anyone who achieved a Ph.D. would be entitled to share in the monies available to humanists. Accord-

---

[1] Louis Kampf, "The Presidential Address" delivered at the 86th Annual Convention of the MLA in Chicago, 27 Dec. 1971. Published as " 'It's Alright, Ma (I'm Only Bleeding)': Literature and Language in the Academy," *PMLA*, 87 (1972), 378.

ing to Foucault, the creation of disciplines with their attendant attendants institutes subjugation; experts administer a closed field of knowledge to *hoi polloi*, allowing a selected few into the enclave. The deconstructive sensibility is too sceptical and ironic to partake wholly of Kampf's utopian rhapsodies; nonetheless, its enemy, too, is the status quo with its inviolable sense of literature and its inflated and revered paraphernalia. In any case, contemporary critics cannot afford to be complacent about either their status or the status of their forays into texts. Their relationship to world and text is an ideological one, laden with implications for the practice of literature and criticism as well as for the shape of the university and other seemingly monolithic institutions.

Although Said, John Reed, Edmund Wilson, F.O. Matthiessen, and Gregory Jay are a salmagundi of critics, none is complacent about his role in or out of the library, in or out of the academy. Said is an esteemed, though dissident, middle-aged professor at Columbia University; John Reed participated in the publishing of *The Masses*, a journal extant in the second decade of the twentieth century, and died scurrying after the Russian Revolution; Edmund Wilson was an iconoclastic critic and belle-lettrist whose life spanned most of this century; F.O. Matthiessen committed suicide in 1950 at the age of forty-eight after having written *American Renaissance*, that seminal work of American studies; Gregory Jay is a young scholar whose work on T.S. Eliot is a revision of his Ph.D. dissertation. Each of the critics mentioned spends a good deal of his critical energy focussing on the social implications of his criticism specifically, as well as the act of criticism generally. As much as the ostensible contents of Matthiessen's *American Renaissance*, Wilson's *Axel's Castle*, and Jay's *T.S. Eliot and the Poetics of Literary History* are concerned with, respectively, mid-nineteenth century American writers, symbolism in early twentieth century literature, and T.S. Eliot, the works are saturated with methodologies, implications, and accountability. Their books reveal that testing epistemological boundaries is as important as defining an author or period.

Said begins *The World, the Text, and the Critic* with an account of a conversation with "an old college friend who worked in the Department of Defense for a period during the Vietnam war" (p. 2). That friend told approbatively of the secretary of defense having Lawrence Durrell's *Alexandria Quartet* on his desk. From this anecdote Said draws the lesson that " . . . you can read classy fiction as well as kill and maim because the cultural world is available for that particular sort of camouflaging, and because cultural types are not supposed to interfere in matters for which the social system has not certified them" (p. 3). Said vigorously denounces the evaluation of criticism as effete, a label which allows it to be dispatched to the periphery. Criticism for him is an "insurrectionary" activity which engages texts that are themselves "worldly," that are themselves "events." The domestication of radical thinkers and their assimilation into a "professionalism," here used as pejoratively as is possible, infuriates him. So, too, does the notion of an inviolable, genteel tradition in which literature is regarded as a handful of masterpieces shared and revered by the cognoscenti who radiate good taste and Arnoldian intelligence. Arnold's frame of reference with its opposition of culture and anarchy, the former embodied in the Arnoldian touchstones, supposedly pithy passages culled from Shakespeare, Dante, and the like, the latter represented by a lack of awareness of so-called great moments in literature, is regarded by Said as especially pernicious. Of that tradition (a clearly demarcated line running from Arnold to Eliot to Lionel Trilling and Frye) Said is scornful, finding in it a narrowness of monumental proportions. He also finds in it a growing irrelevance because of "the diminishing acquiescence and deference accorded to what has been called the Natopolitan world long dominating peripheral regions like Africa, Asia and Latin America" (p. 21).

The pithiest maxim one can offer for Said's notions of literature and criticism can be found in his "Introduction" to *The World, the Text, and the Critic*. He writes, " . . . the moment anything acquires the status of a cultural idol or a commodity, it ceases to be interesting" (p. 30). Such an assertion contradicts most of what traditional criticism sets out to do: create and confirm masterpieces, authors, and national literatures as well as enshrine cultural icons. For Said, criticism is radically other than an Arnoldian, holistic, hagiographical pursuit. "In its suspicion of totalizing concepts, in its discontent with reified objects, in its impatience with guilds, special interests, imperialized fiefdoms, and orthodox habits of mind, criticism is most itself and, if the paradox can be tolerated, most unlike itself at the moment it starts turning into organized dogma" (p. 29). Said's stance here verges on Arrabal's anarchistic statement which is this review's epigraph. It also calls to mind Foucault's truculent definition of his own role as critic, quoted in "Michel Foucault's Touchstones": "Writing only interests me to the extent that it unites itself to the reality of a combat, functioning as an instrument, a tactic . . . . I would like my books to be sorts of scalpels, Molotov cocktails, or minefields and have them carbonize after me in the manner of fireworks."[1]

So much criticism has involved the husbanding of texts and authors not, of course, for their intrinsic value but so that they create fields that then require experts as interpreters and curators. What Pound did to Eliot's *The Waste Land*, criticism should do to the canon. Finding the patterns of imagery, say, in Anthony Trollope's *The Last Chronicle of Barset* – and conventional literary criticism's predisposition to revere works that "have stood the test of time" is nowhere rendered more feckless – leads to the installation of Trollope in a literary firmament that itself is a stylized place. The chronologically structured, British-oriented model, built with such seemingly neutral exegetical components, is regarded by Said as a turgid, conservative enterprise that needs to be revamped.

Such is a summation and extrapolation of Said's attitude in *The World, the Text, and the Critic*. His attacks on "monocentrism" and "ethnocentrism" are given a more militantly political cast in *Orientalism*, in which Said inveighs against the West for its construction, as well as relegation, of orientalism. *The World, the Text, and the Critic*, though, contains a series of discontinuous essays which chiefly give Derrida and Foucault leading roles in the dissemination of the kind of decentring

---

[1] Jean-Louis Ezine [interviewer], "Sur la sellette: Michel Foucault," *Lies Nouvelles Litteraires* 2477 (17 March 1975), p. 3. Excerpt trans. by Pamela Major-Poetzl in *Michel Foucault's Archeology of Western Culture: Toward a New Science of History* (Chapel Hill: Univ. of North Carolina Press, 1983), p. 43.

criticism delineated above. There are some forays into the work of Jonathan Swift and Joseph Conrad and two essays which conclude the volume that reiterate motifs explored in *Orientalism*; the book's power as a critical credo, though, is gained from the "Introduction" as well as from the fifth through tenth essays, one of which, "Criticism Between Culture and System," presents an extended examination of Foucault's and Derrida's value as dissident or deconstructive literary critics.

Both Derrida and Foucault have, of course, become *de rigueur* in American academic circles largely through acolytes such as Hartman, J. Hillis Miller, and Said himself. By no means does this portend the radicalization of junior faculty in university English departments, despite the paucity of jobs and abysmal conditions and salaries for new recruits; rather, it affords a new critical entrée into a glutted field. Said, however, is the most incisive critic in articulating the disruptive dimensions of Foucault's and Derrida's thinking. Although he does not accept their ideas uncritically, Said finds in their writings a confrontational engagement with the order brought about by and to Western culture primarily through universities, their various disciplines, and the custodians of their knowledge. Derrida mainly challenges Western metaphysics with its totalizing, teleological, and positivistic methods and systems, whereas Foucault for the most part attacks institutions and their attendant coteries of professionals. Both find that systems of inclusion and exclusion as well as the definitions of propriety and impropriety act to legitimize content and power.

Said writes explicitly that he is drawn to them because they "propose not only to describe but to produce knowledge of the sort that will fall neither into the prepared molds provided by the dominant culture nor into the wholly predictive forms manufactured by a quasi-scientific method" (p. 182). Neither Foucault nor Derrida is primarily a literary critic *per se* – that, though, is a boundary which each trespasses blithely and purposefully – but both in their abhorrence of the positivist ethos that saturates traditional criticism have been catalysts for deconstruction. Although they write with strikingly different tones, techniques, and focuses, which Said in part enumerates, they produce a "contentious" criticism that violates orthodox

THE POSTMODERN UNIVERSITY

parameters of knowledge. The disruption they produce is scholarly while undermining scholarship; it is also, especially in Derrida's case, unserious while providing a serious threat to profundity. These attributes are extolled by Said who appropriates them in *The World, the Text, and the Critic* and elsewhere to confront seemingly solid edifices of learning. Stridency is unabashedly present in *The World, the Text, and the Critic*. Polemical statements are not infrequent as Said often urges the considerable consequences of a realignment of criticism:

> In the main American literary criticism can afford to shed its partly self-imposed and socially legislated isolation, at least with reference to history and society. There is a whole world manipulated not only by so-called reasons of state but by every variety of ahistorical consumerism, whose ethnocentrism and mendacity promise the impoverishment and oppression of most of the globe. (p. 177)

Kampf, Farber, and even Arrabal are preciously close here – the critic seems to be one step from the barricades.

The founders, publishers, and writers of *The Masses* agitated for a similarly precipitous movement from text to world. They – John Reed, inflated in Warren Beatty's *Reds*, as well as Max Eastman, Emma Goldman, and Floyd Dell, among others – are the subject of Leslie Fishbein's book, *Rebels in Bohemia: The Radicals of 'The Masses,' 1911-1917*. Although Fishbein explores the bohemian and socialist characters and context of *The Masses'* publication, an interesting because turbulent topic, the book itself contains too many compartmentalized and potted biographies and sections. "Radicals," we are told, "longed for a vacation from responsibility . . ." (p. 179); the impact of Nietzsche and European thought is allotted three pages; the consequences of "the sexual revolution" are summarized rather cursorily. Nonetheless, the material Fishbein examines is voluminous – the bibliography is especially rich and extensive; also, she enunciates *The Masses'* direction succinctly. The magazine was "the product of a revolt against the genteel tradition . . ." (p. 15). Its credo was to turn out a revolutionary journal, one "directed against rigidity and dogma wherever it is found" (p. 18).

The magazine's editorial crises, especially concerning the efficacy of art as an aid in the shaping of a political consciousness, are interesting insofar as the scope of this review is concerned. Fishbein understands the editors' debates about art as eddying around two polarities: commitment to social reconstruction ("politically conscious art") and indulgence in bohemian styles ("free expression"). For the most part the editors of *The Masses* appear to have regarded writing dubiously, as an ersatz version of acting or doing, despite the requirement that they have a medium for their work. There is, though, the recognition of the inextricable relation of the world and text: "Changes in the economic and political realm would have to be accompanied by a transformation of culture . . . " (p. 18). Such a situation appears to have frustrated many of *The Masses'* staff and writers who longed for a simpler, more direct implantation of their ideals. They championed wholeheartedly "the cause of anarchists, Industrial Workers of the World, advocates of birth control, and exponents of free love" (p. 18); yet the integration of theory and practice, criticism and commitment they found to be a difficult task. Speculating on the brevity of *The Masses'* run and its inability to leave a strong legacy, Fishbein acknowledges the contribution of the U.S. government which hounded the radical magazine and for a time denied it mailing privileges. She also suggests that disillusionment set in when the easy passage between text and world was seen to be illusory. Criticism, as deconstructionists among others would aver, does not lead directly to social reform. Fishbein, though, writes supportively and nostalgically about an early twentieth century group which had a more innocent sense of the activity: "They attempted a revolutionary transformation of consciousness that would prepare them for the cooperative commonwealth to come. To live as one did before the revolution after the revolution has come truly is to be blessed" (p. 208).

Although it appeared for a time as if Edmund Wilson would succumb to grandiose simplifications, his oeuvre reveals a trenchantly iconoclastic critic who might fulfil Said's notion of the restive, unaccepting critic. *To the Finland Station* and *Travels in Two Democracies*, both written in the thirties, are redolent of what George H. Douglas calls Wilson's faith in some kind of humanitarian socialism. Douglas has, to be sure, read sympathetically and carefully the sizable output of Wilson. From time to time in *Edmund Wilson's America*, indeed, it is difficult to discern when Douglas is paraphrasing Wilson and when he is articulating his own position. For example, Douglas writes: " . . . the reason why we are stymied by bureaucrats, why our minds are befuddled with ideas like 'democracy' that really do not mean much, is that we have lost the superior values and ways of living that once held out hope of a decent civilization" (p. 218). For the most part Douglas's intellectual biography proceeds in such a manner, with a solid, close reading of Wilson's shifting interests, both cerebral and visceral. The writing in *Edmund Wilson's America* is unexceptional and unexceptionable. We glean matter-of-factly and chronologically Wilson's elitist upbringing and education, his attraction to women (which, fortunately, brings into the book Dorothy Parker and her acute wit and one-liners), his utopian visions and his growing disgust with capitalist precepts, and his articulation especially in *Patriotic Gore* of the miasma that America had become. Wilson's scorn for academia specifically and bureaucracies and institutions generally is also traced.

Once again, though, one gets the sense of a literary critic who refuses the attenuated precinct of aesthetics. As Douglas relates, Wilson "did not regard literature and daily social life as being locked into separate compartments with the literary critic being the one who kept his nose clean of things political, his eyes shut to what was going on right down the street" (pp. 82-83). Wilson's disgust with the academic profession stems in part from his sense that the university literary critic is consigned to a ghetto, an apolitical, circumscribed place. His best-known work of literary criticism, writes Douglas, offers a rebuke to early twentieth century writings which Wilson felt were too hermetic, too dandyish. Wilson's bellicosity about the state of American life as well as American letters cannot merely be attributed to his maturation in an era thought to be a highly politicized one. Like Said after him, Wilson is too impassioned about the interaction of world and text to settle for an isolated study of the latter. *Edmund Wilson's America* presents Wilson's life and works in a somewhat formulaic manner; nonetheless, Douglas's subject is interesting enough to carry the reader through the book.

The same could be said of *F.O. Matthiessen: Christian Socialist as Critic*. Frederick C. Stern's subject was a Christian, socialist, and homosexual who wrote one of the most influential works in American studies, *American Renaissance*, before committing suicide in 1950. Stern offers an extended reading (perhaps overly so) of Matthiessen's major works and also delineates his major cultural concerns in a more or less orthodox format. Occasionally Stern provides a more personal point of view by acknowledging Matthiessen's influence on him and others like him, "those of us who thought of ourselves as radicals in the late forties and very early fifties, and as radicals who cared a great deal about literature but could find very few critics among our elders whose work we found inspiring" (p. ix). Despite writing with a narrower and more purely literary focus than Wilson, whose work Matthiessen cites as an influence on him, Matthiessen reveals a concern with language and form, as well as a methodology akin to the New Critics that, nonetheless, is not merely disinterested. Matthiessen writes, " 'An artist's use of language is the most sensitive index to cultural history, since a man can articulate only what he is, and what he has been made by the society of which he is a willing or an unwilling part' " (p. 128). Although his focus is the American writers of literature of the nineteenth and early twentieth centuries, Matthiessen always has broader social concerns as his ultimate focus. Stern, indeed, celebrates Matthiessen as a model because of his belief in the symbiotic relationship between good literature and good society. Stern also refurbishes Matthiessen as an exemplar on a more immediate level. "Scholasticisims" were his enemy as they were Wilson's and Stern sees in his rejection of them a way of mitigating some still current pedagogical problems: "If nothing else, the distinction between mass civilization and minority culture continues to be a problem that faces us daily, as every teacher confronting a new freshman class realizes anew" (p. 244).

The problem of how to be a scholar and activist, to be a bibliophile and an *au courant* figure is the major one that each of the critics examined heretofore has addressed. Lawyers, for instance, confront no such division partly because they translate themselves into the public (i.e., legislative) arena so frequently. Somehow, though, the act of careful, critical reading of literature has been pushed to the periphery of social practices; consequently, the critic has, throughout the twentieth century, it appears, felt himself or herself to be a kind of schizophrenic character balancing personal and collective focuses that could be, but are not, regarded as congruent. Marxist, New Critical, and even deconstructionist critical modes, thought by their early adherents to be laden with the power to transform life as well as art, sink back into the university's milieu as epicene methodologies, their vitality vitiated in academic and professional contexts.

An examination of Gregory S. Jay's *T.S. Eliot and the Poetics of Literary History* yields some insights into this dilemma. Jay's book is saturated with the language of deconstruction. "Logocentrism" and "aporia" are mixed with quotations from Lacan and Derrida, all in the service of a reading of Eliot that undoes a simplistic notion of Eliot's engagement with tradition. However, *T.S. Eliot and the Poetics of Literary History* is not just another book in the prodigious canon of Eliot criticism. Jay writes, " . . . an inquiry into Eliot's theorizing may suggest a reassessment of recent issues in American criticism" (p. 67). Thus, despite a concern with "écriture," supplements, and other lexical treats from the arcana of contemporary literary criticism, Jay's shaping ideology is not very different than Wilson's, or Matthiessen's, or Said's, or even Reed's; he wishes to make the critical act impinge on the reading of the world as much as on the reading of the text. Jay begins his book by writing, "Literary criticism is a kind of naming" (p. 1). "Canonization" and "dismissal" are names which have been attached to Eliot's literary identity and which Jay attempts to rebut. In the wake of his postmodernist re-vision of Eliot's oeuvre we are left with the following definition of literary criticism: "[It] inhabits a postlapsarian world where we resist any final name, though we draw ourselves on in the hopes that our appellations may have a lasting role in shaping what others know and do" (p. 1). There is that messianic zeal again, only this time written deconstructively. Naming in order to un-name or to make conscious the arbitrariness of naming is the critical act of the eighties. However, despite the urgings of Derrida to upset notions of margin and centre, the critical discourse remains on the margin. This, its subversiveness indeed, just may be the source of its health. Or, this may be the only consolation for a marginalized discourse. (In "the real world" people read fiction for diversion and do not read criticism at all.) Since no coup by literary critics appears to be in the offing (they are even losing ground in the ever more pragmatic universities of recent years), solace will in all likelihood only be found in heartfelt books about literature and literary theory.

'Everybody Must Get Stoned' (:)
Reading Thomas Pynchon

"Behind Thomas Pynchon's almost Emersonian faith in the unity of Creation . . ."[1]: thus begins Joseph W. Slade in an article of his dealing with *Gravity's Rainbow*. I deduce from his opening remark that Slade is "stoned." Of course, academia being the genteel milieu that it is, no reproach is meant regarding Slade's character (of which I have no knowledge). The implications of the comment are of a punning nature, less personal even than Jane Gallop's affectionate reference to Jacques Lacan in *The Daughter's Seduction* as a "prick."[2] (A less circumscribed and sanitized vocabulary just might provide the intellectual enema postmodern literary criticism demands; arguments to that end, however, are outside the purview of this essay.) Perhaps a personal anecdote (also usually outré in scholarly publications) will clarify what I mean to be a metaphor regarding Slade's condition. Some years ago I went to see David Bowie in concert. Before he appeared on-stage, people in the stands opposite me held aloft lit matches and lighters – a not infrequent occurrence at rock concerts. It seemed to me, though, that the configurations of the flames offered an outsized pattern such as one sees at American college football games at which students hold up cards in order to spell out their team's nickname, for instance.

Perceiving pattern or order in random accumulations of

---

[1] Joseph W. Slade, "Religion, Psychology, Sex, and Love in *Gravity's Rainbow*," in *Approaches to 'Gravity's Rainbow'*, ed. Charles Clerc (Columbus: Ohio State Univ. Press, 1983), p. 153.

[2] Jane Gallop, *The Daughter's Seduction: Feminism and Psychoanalysis* (Ithaca, N.Y.: Cornell Univ. Press, 1982), p. 36.

words, data, or phenomena is a frequent motif, a dilemma one might say, encountered by Pynchon's characters as well as by readers of his fiction. Was my epiphany at the Bowie performance hallucination, paranoia, or observation? Similarly, is Oedipa's discernment of a sub-cultural Trystero network, or Slothrop's notion that PISCES, the firm, or simply and malignantly "They," are "out to get him," or Stencil's relentless sorting through multiple Vs perception or fantasy? In the inundation of articles on Pynchon and his fiction a congruent scepticism should always work against the critic's apprehension of pattern, insight of whatever kind, in a novel or story by Pynchon. The myriad of details that fill out the texts can be thought of as potentially rather than inherently related. Thus, works examining Pynchon's treatment of economics, information theory, film, war, sex, religion, and love, the last three being Slade's focuses, have the status of projections or paranoid visions as much as of observation for those readers of criticism schooled in Pynchon's ludic manoeuvres. False documents, both critical and novelistic, become blurred with true documents.

Slade's sureness undermines, from a postmodernist perspective, his totalizing, holistic assertion. Perhaps his qualifier, "almost," allows him a relativistic dodge or cancels his meaning entirely as in the *obiter dictum* of Saul in Pynchon's short story "Entropy":

Tell a girl: 'I love you.' No trouble with two-thirds of that it's a closed circuit. Just you and she. But that nasty four-letter word in the middle, *that's* the one you have to look out for. Ambiguity. Redundance. Irrelevance, even. Leakage. All this is noise. Noise screws up your signal, makes for disorganization in the circuit.[1]

The noise in Slade's statement mitigates the severity of his absolutism; regardless, that statement, coming as it does from an astute reader of Pynchon's texts, reveals the difficulty of engaging *V., The Crying of Lot 49,* and *Gravity's Rainbow.* One

---

[1] Thomas Pynchon, "Entropy," in *12 From the Sixties,* ed. R. Kostelanetz (New York: Dell, 1967), p. 29.

has to be aware as a critic that one's clever formulations impose as much as reveal order; moreover, the two tendencies co-exist in a kinetic way so as to retard unitary, summarizing statements about what Pynchon's metaphysical or teleological tendencies are. This kind of ambivalence, deliberately concocted, is, in short, the *raison d'être* of his fiction.

The Crying of Lot 49 could, for example, be explained as a novel in which a character is in search of a plot, with the herculean reader pursuing an analogous detective chase. Like Oedipa Maas (and Joseph W. Slade) understanding is either hallucinatory or revelatory or both. As Oedipa speculates,

> Either you have stumbled indeed, without the aid of LSD or other indole alkaloids, onto a secret richness and concealed density of dream; onto a network by which x number of Americans are truly communicating whilst reserving their lies, recitations of routine, arid betrayals of spiritual poverty, for the official government delivery system; maybe even onto a real alternative to the exitlessness, to the absence of surprise to life, that harrows the head of everybody American you know, and you too, sweetie. Or you are hallucinating it.[1]

It is inescapable to note the omnipotence and ubiquity of "the official government system" – America or, by extension, the whole technocratic-capitalist-totalitarian-industrial complex – that enforces a definitive reading by virtue of its power rather than by the intrinsic, legitimate truth of a text or a culture. That kind of distortion of a dispersed text forces Oedipa to hunt and yearn for a different reading and Slothrop to flee a seemingly suffocating and dictatorial construct. Concomitantly, a narrow, homogeneous critical interpretation of a Pynchon novel implies a similar straitjacketing and hegemony. As the Italian Marxist Antonio Gramsci wrote, "Every relationship of 'hegemony' is

---

[1] Thomas Pynchon, *The Crying of Lot 49* (New York: Bantam, 1982), p. 128. Further quotations from the novel will appear in the text with the designation *Lot* as well as pagination. Quotations from *Gravity's Rainbow* are from the 1973 Viking edition and will appear in the text with the designation *GR* as well as pagination.

necessarily an educational relationship . . . . "[1] Such a hierarchical context, and that includes the acts of teaching and criticism, entails too fixed an interaction between the powerful and the powerless and between experts and the public for Pynchon to be at all sanguine about it.

The second thing to note is the possibility of escape from the inflexibility of mainstream culture that drugs offer; or rather, drugs yield not so much an escape as an alternate route, one which takes one to the "direct, epileptic Word" (*Lot*, p. 87) as it is called in *The Crying of Lot 49* or, in another pithy phrase from the same novel, "pulsing stelliferous Meaning" (*Lot*, p. 58). They conduct one away from a socially enforced reality. Such a lure might remind one of Allen Ginsberg's or Carlos Castaneda's paeans to drugs as a means of bypassing consciousness, of apprehending a transcendental truth. For Ginsberg, restive as he was with the confines of language, drugs undid its ratiocinative properties; poetry could be bardic or prophetic only if it were written in a frenzied way, rejecting the conventions of art and "eluding the last gyzym of consciousness."[2] He asks in "Mescaline," "What can I do to Heaven by pounding on Typewriter/ . . . /I'm going away from the poem . . . . "[3] As he writes in the concluding lines of *Howl*, Part I, his wish is to join "the elemental verbs and set the noun and dash of consciousness together jumping with sensation of Pater Omnipotens Aeterna Deus,"[4] that is, to make everyday language redolent of divine emanations. Being "stoned," chanting "om," and bombarding the reader of his poetry with Whitmanesque lists are ways Ginsberg has sought to extricate himself from language's linearity, to speak the "direct, epileptic Word" which is a wonderfully apt phrase so germane to Ginsberg's enterprise, connoting as it does the word made flesh, signifier joined with signified, word and world yoked together. For the unironic, by

---

[1] Antonio Gramsci, *Selections from the Prison Notebooks*, eds. Quinton Hoare and Geoffrey Nowell Smith (London: Lawrence and Wishart, 1971), p. 350.

[2] Allen Ginsberg, *Howl and Other Poems* (San Francisco: City Lights, 1956), p. 12.

[3] Allen Ginsberg, *Collected Poems: 1947-1980* (New York: Harper and Row, 1984), p. 229.

[4] Ginsberg, *Howl*, p. 16.

no means postmodern Ginsberg (as well as for Castaneda, St. John of the Cross and other mystics) such a by-product of drugs or of altered states induced by other means is their most desirable property. Whatever apprehension of truth, of "stelliferous Meaning," is gleaned in a Pynchon novel by way of drugs, there is always the ironic or palinodic sense that such a perception is not an apocalyptic one, that it is merely a tantalizing consequence of the ingestion of "LSD or other indole alkaloids."

Because criticism is most often performed and regarded as a recuperative act, seemingly at odds with the "Cocaine – or cards?" (GR, p. 517) choice Pynchon appropriates from a Fritz Lang film for Gravity's Rainbow, an incisive response to the deconstructive or dispersive turn of postmodern literature generally and Pynchon's fiction specifically is consistently attenuated. Despite the phalanx of acolytes Derrida, Foucault, and Lacan have acquired, rarely are their aperçus deployed as anything except those of avant-garde authorities. That the binding of a heterogeneous and discontinuous work such as Gravity's Rainbow is an achievement akin to a drug "high" probably chafes traditional scholars' perceptions of their skills and functions. Barbara Johnson in The Critical Difference, however, presents a distinctly postmodern sensibility when she lauds Roland Barthes for his insistence on cultivating the ability "to pluralize the reader's intake, to effect a resistance to the reader's desire to restructure the text into large, ordered masses of meaning."[1] She cites one of Barthes's maxims in S/Z: " . . . we must renounce structuring this text . . . , as was done by classical rhetoric and by secondary-school explication: no construction of the text . . . . "[2] Prohibition of the kind exhibited by Barthes is echoed by Pynchon's techniques. Via tantalizing but ultimately unintegrated details (unless one is "stoned," characters' interaction with one another is a result of an arbitrariness equivalent to a telephone book's compilation), recondite vocabulary, arcane

---

[1] Barbara Johnson, The Critical Difference: Essays in the Contemporary Rhetoric of Reading (Baltimore: Johns Hopkins Univ. Press, 1980), p. 6.

[2] Roland Barthes, S/Z, trans. Richard Miller (New York: Hill and Wang, 1974), pp. 11-12.

and occasionally fabricated allusions, diffuse sentence structure
– by these and other ploys of dispersion Pynchon extends his
"stoned"/sober conundrum.

At one point late in *Gravity's Rainbow* two "minor" characters named Gustav and Andre are smoking hashish out of a
"classical *kazoo*" (*GR*, p. 745). (Hashish, as well as sodium
amytal, opium, and LSD are among the drugs frequently in
evidence in Pynchon's fiction.) That the kazoo is, according to
ex-Peenemünde engineers, the perfect instrument for optimum
inhalation of the drug is merely another tidbit in an exponential
array of Pynchonesque data. It can, of course, be linked with the
description of shopping centre "muzak" found at the beginning
of *The Crying of Lot 49*: " . . . today she came through the
bead-curtained entrance around bar 4 of the Fort Wayne
Settecento Ensemble's variorum recording of the Vivaldi Kazoo
Concerto, Boyd Beaver, soloist, . . . " (*Lot*, p. 2). The kazoo,
innocent instrument of the mundane become an instrument of
the underground, is a comic motif of marginal concern for
Pynchon . . . as long as the reader is comfortable with such a
displacing onto the periphery and thereby providing a hierarchy of effects in the novel (cf. Derrida's *Margins of Philosophy*).
Further to the issue of drugs, though, the hashish smokers have
the added luxury of being able to pull back the rug from the
floor and watch a movie produced by Gerhardt von Göll called
New Dope:

And that's what it's about, a brand new kind of dope
that nobody's ever heard of. One of the most annoying
characteristics of the shit is that the minute you take it
you are rendered incapable of ever telling anybody
what it's like, or worse, where to get any. Dealers are as
in the dark as anybody. All you can hope is that you'll
come across somebody in the act of taking (shooting?
smoking? swallowing?) some. It is the dope that finds
you, apparently. Part of a reverse world whose agents
run around with guns which are like vacuum cleaners
operating in the direction of life – pull the trigger and
bullets are sucked back out of the recently dead into the

93

barrel, and the Great Irreversible is actually reversed as the corpse comes to life to the accompaniment of a backwards gunshot . . . . (*GR*, p. 745)

Such a drug with its ability to reverse procedures, to send one back to origins, is an impossibility. Pynchon's oft-mentioned preterites cannot be erased, returned to beginnings. The "dope," though, promises resolution of and extrication from history.

Although Pynchon's work has its trenchantly political dimensions, here he is indulging in cosmological speculations which have their vital eschatological and metaphysical aspects. Recent theories of avant-garde physicists read as if *their* inventors are "stoned" (in the way in which we have been speaking, of course). These tenuous hypotheses regarding the big bang entail theoretically reversing the process of cosmological history to arrive at "The Beginning." Their notions are articulated by Martin Gardner in a way reminiscent of the "new dope's" faculty of reversing the "Great Irreversible." In what Gardner calls their "supersymmetry theories,"

> . . . immediately after the big bang, when the temperature of the universe was unthinkably high, elegant symmetries prevailed, then were broken as the universe rapidly expanded and cooled. Let's run this script backward in time. When temperature rises to a certain point, electromagnetism and the weak force become one force. Go further back in time, when temperatures are still higher, and the electroweak force fuses with the strong. Go back some more, to less than a nanosecond (one-billionth of a second) after the big bang. All forces are now a single force field, perhaps with a single superparticle.[1]

---

[1] Martin Gardner, "Physics: The End of The Road?" *The New York Review of Books*, 13 June 1985, p. 32.

Juxtaposing the two major quotations above allows one to understand the implications of Pynchon's metaphysics – or rather his scepticism regarding metaphysics, his deconstructive, postmodern turn denying the possibility of origin as well as of order and homogeneity. System and symmetry disappeared a fraction of a second after the big bang; consequently, philosophical framing and comprehending involve tidying and misreading rather than deducing.

Heinz R. Pagels, whose book Gardner is reviewing in the article from which I have quoted, pithily contends that "our universe today is the frozen, asymmetric remnant of its earliest hot state."[1] In fiction as in physics, to coin an apothegm of my own. Unity and a unitary reading which mimetically encapsulate a symmetrical world are only possible *ab origine*, at the beginning of time. Only Gerhardt von Göll's "new dope" allows one the illusion of going backward to that harmonious, pellucid moment, of making the preterite present, just as physicists can only conjecture about an original state which is unlike our contemporary universe; they cannot reinvent or re-present that utopian instant. A nanosecond after the big bang is the only moment at which a comprehensive, synthesizable meaning could be gleaned from the world.

Just as the lack of symmetry is a condition of the universe, it is a condition of texts as well. The "direct, epileptic Word" is not recuperable; therefore, texts must have multifarious, contradictory, asymmetrical meanings. The cosmic and the novelistic are yoked at the beginning of *Gravity's Rainbow* when Pynchon writes, "No, this is not a disentanglement from, but a progressive *knotting into* . . . " (*GR*, p. 3) – in physics as in the novel, the title of which calls the metaphor into play. That, in Coover's formulation, all conceptualizing is a kind of fiction-making and, in Hayden White's maxim, all language is catachresis, are consequences which devolve from Pynchon's embracing the notion of a universe which, if it dances to the music of the spheres, does so in terms of Schoenberg's or Křenek's atonal compositions. Disentanglement would require the "new dope,"

---

[1] Heinz R. Pagels, *Perfect Symmetry: The Search for the Beginning of Time* (New York: Simon and Schuster, 1985). Quoted by Gardner, p. 32.

the reversal of cosmic and social history. "Gerhardt Von Göll Becomes Sodium Amytal Freak!" (*GR*, p. 746) reads one of the titles which flash onto the floor as part of the movie. That drug is also given to Slothrop and is mulled overy by Tchitcherine who identifies it fancifully with the word "black," which, he remembers, runs through Slothrop's transcript. He then ruminates on this motif:

> Is there a single root, deeper than anyone has probed, from which Slothrop's Blackwords only appear to flower separately? Or has he by way of the language caught the German mania for name-giving, dividing the Creation finer and finer, analyzing, setting namer more hopelessly apart from named, even to bringing in the mathematics of combination, tacking together established norms to get new ones, the insanely, endlessly diddling play of a chemist whose molecules are words . . . . (*GR*, p. 391)

Here in terms of language, actually a poststructuralist primer, is the same notion of a progressive knotting into with which Pynchon begins the novel. The sodium amytal produced an hallucinogenic flow of words which Tchitcherine, who is himself described as susceptible to the drug's effect, first reads as the blackness that precedes language, then as a cooled and asymmetrical prison-house in which signifier and signified are irreparably severed. Inspissated meanings are drug-induced or spiritualist ones and in *Gravity's Rainbow* their authors, drug-takers or system-makers, litter the Platz. In that locale are those who take morning-glory seeds as well as "stumblebum magicians who can't help leaving themselves wide open for disastrous visits from Qlippoth, Ouija-board jokesters, poltergeists, all kinds of astral-plane tankers and feebs" and also "devotees of the I Ching" (*GR*, p. 746). The search backward through language is shortcircuited by the "feebs" et al., who are restive with and suspicious of language. History and historians have not written a palindrome where return to the beginning is a condition of the construct. Incidentally, about the above mentioned devotees of Chinese hexagrams Pynchon jokes that they have "a favourite hexagram tattooed on each toe, . . . [and] can never stay in one place for long, can you guess why? Because they always have I Ching feet!" (*GR*, p. 746) His punning is a deliberate attempt to trap cosmic systems in the labyrinth of language.

Derrida has enunciated the postmodernist credo thusly: "In the beginning is hermeneutics."[1] There is no moment (except one nanosecond after the big bang) that is outside language, that resolves itself into something decipherable, something that can be read singly, transparently, that need not be reread, that resolves itself into a constant, fully integrated message. That art can provide a consummate metaphor or produce a mimetic text is, therefore, a false premise. In *The Crying of Lot 49* Pynchon offers the counsel of a painting by "the beautiful Spanish exile Remedios Varo" called "Bordando el Manto Terrestre." It is a triptych portraying a few girls embroidering a tapestry "which spilled out the slit windows and into a void, seeking hopelessly to fill the void" (*Lot*, p. 10). Oedipa stands before the painting and cries, realizing the impossibility of art's quest of uniting or reflecting the world. It is, nonetheless, part of the human condition to try to read the world's signs which are a complex and shifting, elusive and unresolvable group of signifiers. For Pynchon, as for Derrida, the blank page or a non-semiotic world can only be thought of in terms of that non-recuperable nanosecond. Life after that moment is difference, dispersion. The blackness Tchitcherine thinks of is absence, death; thus it is presented as a horror in all Pynchon's fiction. *Gravity's Rainbow*, an ultimately diffuse, promiscuous, excessive work (its joy lying in its messiness, if you will) ends not with the terror involved with excess, but with that bound up with death, with a lack of signifiers, because such a condition bespeaks only the non-human, the unthinkable.

The last scene of the novel deals with a movie audience uneasy with absence. "The screen is a dim page spread before us, white and silent . . . . And in the darkening and awful expanse of screen something has kept on, a film we have not

---

[1] Jacques Derrida, *Writing and Difference*, trans. Allan Bass (Chicago: Univ. of Chicago Press, 1978), p. 67.

learned to see . . . . And it is just here, just at this dark and silent frame, that the pointed tip of the Rocket . . . " (*GR*, p. 760). Here the novel is about to end with the rocket about to hit the theatre. Blackness and whiteness are brought together to invoke the horror of silence, of the blank page (which ironically yet naturally follows upon the novel's closing). The ultimate rocket, remember, which is often referred to, is numbered 00000, itself connoting *nothing*. Excess and promiscuity for Pynchon, then, a multiplicity of signs and even indulgence in prolixity (one of the complaints often mentioned about *Gravity's Rainbow*), are vitally incorporated in his novels because they are indications of living. Signs laden with totalizing, totalitarian significance and a lack of signs are both heinous. The pleasures of the text inhere in its sprawling, unkempt qualities.

In *Erring: A Postmodern A/theology* Mark C. Taylor, a professor of religious studies, seeks to find religious value in such plurality and amplitude. He writes about incarnation that it is "not a once-and-for-all event, restricted to a specific time and place and limited to a particular individual. Rather, inscription is a continual (though not necessarily a continuous) process."[1] Taylor finds his religious meanings where Barthes finds erotic bliss, *jouissance*. Pynchon has no messianic urge akin to Taylor's; however, both agree on the attractiveness of language's plenitude and on its totalitarian aspects if that plenitude is minimized. Exuberance regarding language's indeterminacy and its possibilities, as well as culture's indeterminacy and possibilities, protrudes from Pynchon's mammoth text, both in terms of content and form. About the Rocket 00000, for instance, Pynchon writes, "Beyond simple steel erection, the Rocket was an entire system *won*, away from the feminine darkness, held against the entropies of lovable but scatterbrained Mother Nature . . . " (*GR*, p. 324). The rocket organizes and systematizes, distorting thereby a rich world which Pynchon calls "scatterbrained." Similarly, late in the novel he writes pejoratively about people, to whom he refers as "God's spoilers," accusing them of bringing death in terms of the limiting of an abundance

---

[1] Mark C. Taylor, *Erring: A Postmodern A/theology* (Chicago: Univ. of Chicago Press, 1984), p. 104.

of meanings. They "are meant only to look at [the world] dead, in still strata, transputrefied to oil or coal. Alive, it was a threat: it was Titans, was an overpeaking of life so clangorous and mad, such a green corona about Earth's body that some spoiler *had* to be brought in . . . " (*GR*, p. 720). Such beings who employ simplification and reductiveness Pynchon refers to as counter-revolutionaries.

Pynchon's lists, his data, are meant to separate and discriminate, unlike the lists of, say, Walt Whitman or Allen Ginsberg, mystics both, which are used in an incantatory way to speak of harmony and integration. (Note, too, in a congruent vein the incessant listing Donald Barthelme employs to forestall easy passage from words to abstract concepts.) Trying to link the various data, the reader, inundated with connections, must falsify them in order to give them a taxonomy; moreover, were he or she to find pattern in all of the words and signs, his or her circuits would be overloaded and, like Oedipa, his/her mind would "blaze out, destroying its own message irreversibly" (*Lot*, p. 69).

Being "stoned" allows one to circumvent the problem by fostering visions, but drug highs along with paranoia and education (with its dichotomies, disciplines, and experts) promote only an illusory enlightenment or epiphany. Once again a drug scene presents Pynchon with the occasion for a disquisition akin to the one just formulated on the lure of drugs. Wimpe and Tchitcherine "shoot up" and the narrator then discourses in an erudite but specious vein (pardon!) on the properties of a drug called "Oneirine." This drug occasionally and selectively produces paranoia of which Pynchon writes, "Like other sorts of paranoia, it is nothing less than the onset, the leading edge, of the discovery that *everything is connected*, everything in the Creation, a secondary illumination – not yet blindingly One, but at least connected, and perhaps a route In . . . " (*GR*, p. 703). If one of Derrida's techniques is the deployment of writing *sous rature*, under erasure, and if Robbe-Grillet writes, it might be said, with *une gomme*, an eraser, both experimentally generating meanings and the erasure of those meanings, Pynchon produces his own palinode, his own assertion and retraction. Dubious modes of gaining insight are all he offers; moreover, these he places in tenuous contexts. Necessary and unnecessary, apocalyptic and parodic, seminal and peripheral – these seeming dualities are introduced so as to render shaky the status of each. Even progression in the text is given to the reader in a way which undermines it: "You will want cause and effect. All right" (GR, p. 663). Teleology and metaphysics, given only perfunctory assent, are unwritten by anarchism and deconstruction.

Any order, then, is an enforced order, and Pynchon, forever sympathetic to subversion and revolution, has Oedipa, for one, search for "another mode of meaning behind the obvious, or none" (Lot, p. 137). In political terms the obvious meaning is a dictated, totalitarian one; on an intellectual level it is a jejune, feckless one. In words which explicitly call forth Oedipa's plaintive cry, Pynchon in Gravity's Rainbow links the need of "seeking other orders behind the visible" (GR, p. 188) with paranoia. Drugs may only appear to provide cosmic intuition, but they, along with other untraditional modes of evasion, allow the search for an unorthodox engagement with and the possible overthrow of reality. No utopia is perceived or created – the nanosecond has passed; nonetheless, receptivity to the dispersion of the world as text is the richest mode Pynchon offers. Received notions, truths, doxa are all vitiated by such a sensibility.

Oedipa's herculean hunting and her insistent, pertinacious readings and rereadings can be regarded as themselves vital: " . . . she wondered if the gemlike 'clues' were only some kind of compensation. To make up for her having lost the direct, epileptic Word . . . " (Lot, p. 87). These clues, hints, signs, intimations never crystallize into ultimate meaning, "the central truth itself, which must somehow each time be too bright for her memory to hold . . . leaving an overexposed blank when the ordinary world came back" (Lot, p. 69). Again, excess is pitted against blankness which is a non-textualized entity, that is to say a deathly one. In one of those tours de force that makes Gravity's Rainbow such a marvellous and marvellously excessive novel (other seemingly gratuitous jeux d'esprit include "the

Mother Conspiracy" and the story of "Byron the Bulb"), Pynchon encapsulates this motif of cluttered writing and ahistorical perfection in terms of a brief haircutting scene:

> Each long haircut is a passage. Hair is yet another kind of modulated frequency. Assume a state of grace in which all hairs were once distributed perfectly even, a time of innocence when they fell perfectly straight, all over the colonel's head. Winds of the day, gestures of distraction, sweat, itchings, sudden surprises, three-foot falls at the edge of sleep, watched skies, remembered shames, all have since written on that perfect grating. Passing through it tonight, restructuring it, Eddie Pensiero is an agent of History. (*GR*, p. 643)

For Taylor grace is mazed in language, in history. Here, Pynchon playfully renders the plurality of signs that grow incrementally as the agents that have altered the hairs on the Colonel's head. The assumption of a state of grace is another of those Pynchonesque accommodations with a religious framework that could as easily stand as a metaphor for physics, the big bang and its fragmentation of a symmetrical state. Everything, even the Colonel's head, is textualized, disordered. Eddie Pensiero, inadequate to the task of full restoration, is thus an agent of continued writing.

History, for Pynchon, contributes accretions; moreover, the act of writing history merely adds to the accretions, producing at best (or for Pynchon, at worst) an arbitrary arrangement of data. Claude Lévi-Strauss's assessment of that activity is apposite at this point. In *The Savage Mind* he writes:

> Even history which claims to be universal is still only a juxtaposition of a few local histories within which (and between which) very much more is left out than is put in .... In so far as history aspires to meaning, it is doomed to select regions, periods, groups of men and individuals in these groups and to make them stand out, as discontinuous figures, against a continuity bare-

ly good enough to be used as a backdrop. A truly total history would cancel itself out – its product would be nought.[1]

Despite the impossibility of writing the world's history, which would be the product of a kind of Funes the Memorius figure – Borges's fabrication who can record all but can conceptualize nothing – Pynchon conflates a plethora of actual and invented figures, events, scientific hypotheses, and places in *Gravity's Rainbow* to present a problem for the reader akin to that of producing a history. To complicate matters further he sometimes lays out his materials in a sequential manner and other times in an aleatory one. *The Crying of Lot 49*, for instance, concludes arbitrarily with a stamp auction that makes sense only because the title is so named and perhaps because the tracking of the legacy of Pierce Inverarity may be the search for the kind of valuable, flawed stamp known as an inverse rarity – name, not intrinsic action, here conferring meaning.

As Pynchon writes of Oedipa's fright when being pinned down by an erratically flying punctured bottle of hair spray, "The can knew where it was going, she sensed, or something fast enough, God or a digital machine, might have computed in advance the complex web of its travel . . . " (*Lot*, p. 23). Just as any macrocosmic history is impossible to write, so too is it impossible to schematize anything complex. Persons' minds are too limited to be able to do what "God or a digital machine" can perform. Pynchon's fascination with entropy, already incisively explored by Anne Mangel in "Maxwell's Demon, Entropy, Information: *The Crying of Lot 49*,"[2] results from the link between information and entropy. The informational content of a message is proportional to the number of permutations and combinations of its symbols. Maximum information occurs when the signs are dispersed in an entropic or fully random state; however, like Funes the Memorius or Lévi-Strauss's unrealizable cosmic historian, the one who understands such

---

[1] Claude Lévi-Strauss, *The Savage Mind*, trans. unnamed (Chicago: Univ. of Chicago Press, 1966), p. 257.

[2] This article appeared in *Tri-Quarterly*, No. 20 (Winter 1971), pp. 194-208.

maximal content is nowhere to be found. Such a person would have to connect too many disparate entities. As Pynchon explains in *Gravity's Rainbow*, "There was no difference between the behavior of a god and the operations of pure chance" (*GR*, p. 323), because both include all possibilities, but neither can be comprehended or schematized. Pynchon's attractiveness, incidentally, to the advocates of artificial intelligence such as Douglas Hofstadter and Richard Dennett stems from his sense of humanity's sorting and intellectual limitations. For the devotees of AI, the human mind is only degrees greater than sophisticated computers which, like vibrators, can do things faster than humans once the code has been mastered. Pynchon's prolixity, his abundant, overloaded novels, then, defy a supreme sorting that would dilute their potential informational content. This is so because to be able to reduce his created world would be to descry a relatively simplistic structure, this given the intellectual capabilities of men and women alluded to above. The number of permutations and combinations in *Gravity's Rainbow* remains deliberately beyond the reader's ken, tantalizing but eluding him or her.

Of course, James Joyce in *Finnegans Wake* creates a labyrinth that for him reflects the modern world, one which demands a rigorous, complex reading. He writes, "(Stoop) if you are abcedminded, to this claybook, what curios of signs (please stoop), in this allaphbed! Can you rede ... its world? It is the same told of all. Many. Miscegenations on miscegenations."[1] In his punning, inventive language Joyce yokes the reading of world and words. Recognizing that " ... the world, mind, is, was and will be writing its own wrunes ... ,"[2] again with the clever dualities tying books and nature, internal and external signs, Joyce makes the reading of *Finnegans Wake* a demanding task. Nonetheless, despite the realization that " ... you need hardly spell me how every word will be bound over to carry three score and ten toptypsical readings ... ,"[3] there isn't in Joyce's fiction the sense that meanings dissolve, retract, frag-

---

[1] James Joyce, *Finnegans Wake* (New York: Viking, 1968), p. 18.

[2] Joyce, p. 19.

[3] Joyce, p. 20.

ment, that they deny scholarly entrees. It is, rather, Joyce's awesome quest (see the thousands of pages of notes that were preparatory to the writing of *Ulysses* and *Finnegans Wake*) to acknowledge and present the loading of language as well as the denial of easy reading and interpretation, while concomitantly offering parallels between and integration of ancient and modern, Hebraic and Hellenic, spiritual and sensual (among other antinomies dealt with). What Joyce in *Finnegans Wake* calls "Gutenmorg,"[1] the descent into history and writing, is not, despite the pun, a place of no transcendence.

In Pynchon's fiction, on the contrary, transcendence is tendered only to the possessed ("stoned," paranoid, or scholarly) who are artificers of a more vulnerable sort than Joyce. The acts of organizing and of hewing meaning from inchoate reality are recompense insofar as they are activities, not end-products. Oedipa Maas, a postmodern version of the classical quester, relentlessly scours places and texts to discern the nebulous Trystero. Only Maxwell's Demon (and perhaps James Joyce), a favoured figure for Pynchon appearing as it does in *The Crying of Lot 49* and *Gravity's Rainbow*, can set the world into "pulsing stelliferous Meaning." Oedipa, unlike Oedipus, is unsure of consequences which ensue from actions that may or may not have causative features. Of Maxwell's Demon Pynchon writes that it attempts "to concentrate energy into one favored room of the Creation at the expense of everything else" (*GR*, p. 411). Such an act for the postmodernist, Pynchon especially, is catachrestic. History disorders, humanity inadequately deciphers. This situation, however, is less vile than the blank page, death, which in *Gravity's Rainbow* threatens via an arsenal of rockets.

Pynchon perplexes the reader not comfortable with the postmodern sensibility, the one without sympathy for the deconstructive turn. If Donald Barthelme's *Snow White* usurps and deflates the force of mythology and folktales as well as the force of archetypal or mythopoeic criticism, whereas *Ulysses* fosters and rewards these forces, Pynchon's texts tease one who marvels at and accedes to the architectonics of Joyce's texts.

---

[1] Joyce, p. 20.

Gravity's Rainbow, The Crying of Lot 49, and to a lesser degree *V.* are replete with the puns, erudition, and legerdemain of *Ulysses* and *Finnegans Wake* while they undo the neatness and orderliness of these constructions. That is, of course, unless you are "stoned" to the extent that these devices not only saturate but also bind Pynchon's wor(l)ds. You would then be viewing the world from the vantage point of one nanosecond after it began.

Palinodes and Palindromes

An interesting phenomenon in contemporary fiction, or at least that strain of it variously called metafiction, surfiction, or postmodernism, is the proliferation of palinodes and palindromes, both literal and figurative. In *Letters*, for instance, Jerome Bray writes that he longs to discover history's palindrome. In *Snow White*, Paul is said to be "writing a palinode." " 'Perhaps it is wrong to have favorites among the forms,' he reflected. 'But retraction has a special allure for me. I would wish to retract everything, if I could, so that the whole written world would be. . . .' "[1] Certainly, retraction has a special allure for those writers who eschew linear, sequential narrative, what might be called teleological fiction; who reject the notion that language is a window onto the world; who are sensitive to the poststructuralist tenet enunciated by Michel Foucault in "The Discourse on Language" that discourse is not a neutral conduit between reality and its meaning.

Retraction, then, is a way of debunking the whole theory of representation: "Representation . . . is *embarrassed figuration*, encumbered with other meanings than that of desire: a space of alibis (reality, morality, likelihood, readability, truth, etc.)."[2] The palinode and palindrome, in which one ends where one begins, are excellent media of retraction. In them nothing has been displaced; all has been erased, and this without disappearing. In the palinode one writes or says something, then one denies it; in the palindrome one traverses a series of letters only to turn around when one reaches the end of that series in order to

---

[1] Donald Barthelme, *Snow White* (New York: Atheneum, 1972), p. 13.

[2] Roland Barthes *The Pleasure of the Text*, trans. Richard Miller (New York: Hill and Wang, 1975), p. 56.

return to the beginning. Thus, despite the expenditure of a great deal of energy, the utterance of a great many words, cancellation has occurred in both cases and meaning is deliberately nullified. What is operant here is, of course, antithetical to the notion of return T.S. Eliot articulates near the conclusion of *Four Quartets*:

We shall not cease from exploration
And the end of all our exploring
Will be to arrive where we started
And know the place for the first time.[1]

For Eliot, circularity involves progression; it entails a quest that may carry the protagonist back to where he or she began, but produces added acumen or insight. Retraction is not the allure. Nor is it the attraction for Jerry in Albee's *The Zoo Story* who utters, " . . . sometimes it's necessary to go a long distance out of the way in order to come back a short distance correctly . . . . "[2] Again in this case return to the beginning implies a new beginning (even if in Jerry's case that new beginning contributes to the end of his life). The classical notion of communication, of writing as communication, is still pertinent to the two writers just cited.

Cancellation and retraction are more relevant to a work such as Beckett's *Waiting for Godot*; about one incident in the play Beckett has said, "I take no sides. I am interested in the shape of ideas. There is a wonderful sentence in Augustine: 'Do not despair; one of the thieves was saved. Do not presume; one of the thieves was damned.' That sentence has a wonderful shape."[3] Indeed, much of *Waiting for Godot*, not merely the anecdotal way in which Vladimir and Estragon debate the merits of the Augustinian condundrum, appears to be structured figuratively as a palinode. There are, for example, Lucky's

---

[1] T.S. Eliot, *Collected Poems, 1909-1962* (London: Faber and Faber, 1963), p. 222.

[2] Edward Albee, *The American Dream and The Zoo Story* (New York: Signet, 1961), p. 30.

[3] As quoted by Ruby Cohn in *Casebook on Waiting for Godot*, ed. Ruby Cohn (New York: Grove, 1967), p. 51.

volubility, then his muteness; the conclusion of Act I being recapitulated but revered in Act II; the giving birth astride the grave, at first lingeringly then instantaneously. Even in *Waiting for Godot* specifically and Beckett's work generally, however, the notion of cancellation or erasure is slightly divergent from the Derridean notion of erasure that makes the deployment of palinodes and palindromes so congenial to fiction writers who are in the Borgesian or Nabokovian, that is to say, the metafictive mold.

Beckett's tendency to retract meaning can be captured in the equation, language equals silence. Silence in all of Beckett's works assumes a seminal place, undermining and subsuming words, signalling their futility. In *The Dismemberment of Orpheus*, Ihab Hassan aptly summarizes Beckett's engagement with language and silence as follows: "[Beckett] listens endlessly to a solipsist drone. Words appear . . . on the page only to declare themselves invalid. We have crossed some invisible line . . . . Postmodern literature moves . . . toward the vanishing point."[1] The subliminal desire to escape the prison house of language, to remove oneself from a language that has been overwhelmed by the cataclysmic events of the twentieth century, is for Hassan the source not only of Beckett's art, but also of Genet's and Hemingway's.

The impulse to create palinodes or palindromes, though, derives from a greater sense of textuality, of "écriture," from, in other words, a more print-oriented engagement with the world than is acknowledged by those writers, Beckett included, whom Hassan defines as prefiguring postmodernism. For Derrida, "to be is to-be-in-the-book,"[2] to be enmeshed in the "necessary *exchange* of one's existence with or for the letter."[3] Transcendence, mimesis, representation – all are specious and illusory. These concepts are also vitiated by the postmodernists who use palinodes and palindromes.

---

[1] Ihab Hassan, *The Dismemberment of Orpheus: Toward a Postmodern Literature* (New York: Oxford Univ. Press, 1971), p. 23.

[2] Jacques Derrida, *Writing and Difference*, trans. Alan Bass (Chicago: Univ. of Chicago Press, 1978), p. 76.

[3] Derrida, p. 70.

Just as punning and other forms of language play are staples of Derrida's technique (and are seminal to his antimetaphysical notion of what philosophy can do), so are similar displays of legerdemain central to postmodern fiction. For both poststructuralists and postmodernists, " . . . the world is in all its parts a cryptogram to be constituted or reconstituted through poetic inscription or deciphering . . . . "[1] Instead of referentiality or transparency, one is left with cryptograms, with language games. In the case of postmodern fiction, one is also left with the grin of Nabokov's cheshire cat which, Ross Wetzsteon writes in his memoir of Nabokov as teacher, the Russian émigré drew in his lectures to mock and subvert the thematic approach to literature. By subjecting various words to "erasure," Derrida seeks to rid them of their metaphysical significance; by constructing their fiction along the lines of palinodes and palindromes, postmodernists aspire to the same goal.

By positing two contradictory endings, John Fowles creates a palinodic structure in *The French Lieutenant's Woman*, Julio Cortázar constructs *Hopscotch* similarly – he provides a chapter grid in his Author's Note by which the reader can "hopscotch" through the novel (Chapter 73 to Chapter 1 to Chapter 2 and so forth) in defiance of the linear chapter sequence; in that way, Cortázar produces two novels both of which cancel one another. The Moebius strip which John Barth uses to frame *Lost in the Funhouse* has a palindromic quality, returning the reader to the beginning and thereby keeping him or her from progressing through the stories. Robbe-Grillet's *The Erasers* can be read as a sustained palinode, erasure, as Bruce Morrissette and other explicators of the novel have written, being at work deconstructing both detective thriller and Oedipus myth. Robbe-Grillet uses much the same method in *In The Labyrinth*: he begins the novel with the sentences, "I am alone here now, under cover. Outside it is raining, . . ." only to write in the following sentence, "Outside the sun is shining. . . ."[2] In short stories such

---

[1] Derrida, p. 76.

[2] Alain Robbe-Grillet, *Two Novels: Jealousy and In the Labyrinth*, trans. by Richard Howard (New York: Grove, 1965), p. 141.

as "The Babysitter" and "The Elevator," Coover projects then cancels numerous storylines, this device being the dominant element in those stories. A more convoluted use of a palinodic structure can be seen in Thomas Pynchon's fiction: in *The Crying of Lot 49*, Oedipa Maas is given the problem of solving the labyrinthine dealings of Pierce Inverarity, a name the lineage of which is "inverse rarity." Also, Metzger, an early accomplice, and Oedipa watch on television a film, *Cashiered*, in which some of the reels are played in reverse order; in *Gravity's Rainbow* the novel, replete with rocket detonations and landings at the beginning, ends with the rocket launching that refers one back to the first sentence in which "a screaming comes across the sky."[1]

Even Joseph Heller, regarded as far more traditional than most of the above-mentioned writers, employs methods I have defined as palinodic. In *Catch-22*, there is Yossarian's stint in the hospital where he works as a censor, playfully blacking out or deleting words in the letters of others until whole pages are obliterated. In *Something Happened* and *Good as Gold*, though, Heller maintains the motif of cancellation thematically, while he begins to work it more deftly into the plot framework of these two novels which are much less episodic than *Catch-22*. Nothing tumultuous happens in *Something Happened* until the narrator, so steeled for something eventful to happen, *makes* it happen out of nothing. In *Gold as Gold*, Heller uses the palinodic technique extensively. Meeting his stepmother for the first time the narrator, Bruce Gold, engages in the following dialogue with her:

"And what," he said in his most courtly manner, "would you like us to call you?"

"I would like you to treat me as my own children do," Gussie Gold replied with graciousness equal to his own. "I would like to think of you all as my very own children. Please call me Mother."

---

[1] Thomas Pynchon, *Gravity's Rainbow* (New York: Viking, 1973), p. 3.

"Very well, Mother," Gold agreed. "Welcome to the family."
"I'm not your mother," she snapped.[1]

Most of the conversations, especially those between Gold and Ralph Newsome, who is on the staff of the president, proceed with deliberate and consistent cancellation of meaning. After Gold tells Newsome that he cannot be bought, the latter responds, " 'We wouldn't want you if you could be, Bruce. . . . This President doesn't want yes-men. What we want are independent men of integrity who will agree with all our decisions after we make them. You'll be entirely on your own.' "[2] In addition, *Good as Gold* concludes with Gold speculating on where he could begin to write the book on Jewish life in America which has already been written and in which he has been featured.

Jerome Bray wants to discover a world as highly structured as a palindrome, what might be called history's palindrome; in seeking the key to the whole cryptogram, he searches for the master plan to the whole prison house of language. As long as such epical keys are regarded as elusive, if not nonexistent, postmodernist fiction makers cultivate aesthetic pleasure by creating cryptogrammic forms such as palinodes and palindromes which allow them to write both something and nothing, simultaneously to construct and deconstruct. At the same time they deny any totalizing engagement with what Derrida calls the structurality of structure: " . . . the structurality of structure . . . has always been neutralized or reduced, and this by a process of giving it a centre or referring it to a point of presence, a fixed origin. The function of this centre was . . . above all to make sure that the organizing principle of the structure would

---

[1] Joseph Heller, *Good as Gold* (New York: Simon and Schuster, 1979), p. 27.
[2] Heller, p. 53.

limit what we might call *freeplay* of the structure."[1] Palinodes and palindromes are, like puns, manifestations of freeplay, not *les règles du jeu*, the rules of the game.

---

[1] Jacques Derrida, "Structure, Sign, and Play in the Discourse of the Human Sciences," in *The Languages of Criticism and the Sciences of Man: The Structuralist Controversy*, eds. Richard Macksey and Eugenio Donato (Baltimore: Johns Hopkins Univ. Press, 1970), pp. 247-48.

The Ludic Temperament
of John Barth

A Reader to the Author of the Author. Unbidden, extending the debate about the postmodern novel (whether it be in a state of 'exhaustion' or 'replenishment'); descrying, as he initiates his argument, a Barth, -es, -elme conspiracy against several drolls and screamers, among them John Gardner, Mary McCarthy, and Leslie Fiedler (and vice versa); defining the Author's sensibility as ludic and relating it to poststructuralism and to the fantastic.

There is no Burlingame-Cook-Castine revolutionary-reactionary confusion among the participants who have debated the merits of postmodern fiction, the kind you and Coover, and Pynchon, and Gass, among others, write. You can, needless to say, fight your own battles, indeed have already excoriated Gardner, reducing his *On Moral Fiction* to "an exercise in literary kneecapping that lumps modernists and postmodernists together without distinction and consigns us all to Hell with the indiscriminate fervor characteristic of late converts to the right." [1] Still, as a combative sort who chafes against his assignment to teach rather than to do, I wish to join the fray, especially since Mary McCarthy, no kin to Eldridge Cleaver, includes me and my ilk as part of the problem rather than the solution: she derides "reviewers and teachers of literature, who, as always, are the reader's main foe." [2] Her primary gripe, though, in *Ideas and the Novel* is with you "goys" who, unlike Roth, Bellow, and Malamud, don't have the "chutzpah" to juggle ideas in full view of the public.

---

[1] John Barth, "The Literature of Replenishment: Postmodernist Fiction," *The Atlantic Monthly*, Jan. 1980, p. 67.

[2] Mary McCarthy, *Ideas and the Novel* (New York: Harcourt, Brace, Jovanovich, 1980), p. 121.

Then there is Leslie Fiedler, who tepidly summarizes his "engagement" with your latest novel in the following way: " ... I have tried recently, with some difficulty, to read my way through John Barth's *Letters* .... "[1] He also maintains that while countless students chorused that *Jonathan Livingston Seagull* changed their lives, nary a one was overheard to say that *Lost in the Funhouse* catalyzed him or her in like manner. Now it is true that my mother would never have let you marry my sister, and that *Letters* is a long read; however, the contentions of Gardner, McCarthy, and Fiedler that your novels (and those of Coover, et al.) disdain ideas or content, and, moreover, are a bad read, demand refutation. Take the latter claim: Fiedler goes so far as to yearn for the halcyon days of the eighteenth and nineteenth centuries in which a work such as Richardson's *Clarissa* (and works by Dostoevski and Tolstoy) could be read " 'with equal pleasure in the kitchen, the parlor and the nursery.' "[2] (Fiedler appropriates this phrase from Emerson.) Perhaps this large still book, as Tennyson referred to it, comfortably companioned the protracted preparation of, say, gâteau St. Honore, but I am somewhat sceptical. Perhaps I merely live in the twentieth century, to quote Richard Brautigan, and would rather read about olive-by-olive orgasms than tenuously and metaphorically be offered olive branches, but this would certainly be a jaundiced interpretation.

My point is a simple one: surely *Letters* (and *The Public Burning* and *JR* and *Gravity's Rainbow*) are as engrossing and compelling and even as readable as *Clarissa*. A hyperthyroid novel is, of course, a hyperthyroid novel and demands an extended commitment on the part of the reader. Because that novel might not provide a teleological context within which to move from word to word and page to page does not necessarily hamper its readability. Or in Gass's metaphor: "Only a literalist at loving would expect to plug ahead like the highway people's line machine, straight over hill and dale .... "[3] Or to advance

---

[1] Leslie A. Fiedler, "The Death and Rebirths of the Novel," *Salmagundi*, No. 50-51 (1980-81), p. 144.

[2] Fiedler, p. 145.

[3] William Gass, *Willie Masters' Lonesome Wife* (New York: Knopf, 1971), n.p.

the issue another way, is Jackson Pollock's *Mural* any less appreciable or viewable than Constable's *Hay Wain?* Of course not. What is asked of the reader is that he or she bring to the avant-garde work the following: a different set of expectations, a willingness to deconstruct traditional texts, and a recognition that clichéd modes of writing are not sacrosanct. The willing suspension of disbelief can be yoked to form as well as to content. These demands have been made before: *vide* Robert Browning's *Sordello*, which nearly drove Leigh Hunt to a relapse of the nervous disorder he had just overcome; also, Robert Bridges's hesitation about publishing Gerard Manley Hopkins' poetry because of its radical technical departures from mainstream verse, nineteenth century variety.

You have said on different occasions that no one would think of building the Chartres Cathedral nowadays, that the first half of the twentieth century did happen – "and there's no going back to Tolstoy and Dickens & Co. except on nostalgia trips."[1] Sterne and Joyce and Flann O'Brien and Virginia Woolf as well as your postmodern contemporaries have, I would hope, prepared people to read your fiction which in turn has prepared people to read the works of Frederic Tuten, Walter Abish, and Eric McCormack. You state the case, it seems to me, with forbearance and acuity when you write:

> If the modernist, carrying the torch of romanticism, taught us that linearity, rationality, consciousness, cause and effect, naive illusionism, transparent language, innocent anecdote, and middle-class moral conventions are not the whole story, then from the perspective of these closing decades of our century we may appreciate that the contraries of these things are not the whole story either.[2]

Occasionally, you have seemed to be less temperate, jocularly accusing your readers of being print-oriented bastards, but your

---

[1] Barth, p. 70.
[2] Barth, p. 70.

purpose is a vital, appropriate, and, indeed, an heuristic one: to teach readers the mechanics of fiction.

You engage in your fiction questions such as: What are its conventions? How does one read it? What is its ontological status? Moreover, you often engage these questions directly. Truffaut, speaking of the traditional cinema, once said: "Intelligence stayed *behind* the camera; it didn't try to be in evidence on the screen."[1] You and the other postmodernists have decided to move out of the closet, so to speak, and onto the page, to explore the aesthetics of the novel with immediacy and boldness. You may be interested to know that your fiction is excellent in the service of pedagogy. Because it "foregrounds" technique and language it forces students to examine the distinctive characteristics of fiction rather than to pursue now vapid examinations of plot, character, and theme, all of which can be studied on *extra*-literary terrains. I tell students who are recalcitrant of being weaned to do character sketches of their classmates and to read novels the way Nabokov as teacher and novelist suggested: "Caress the details," he uttered, meaning the language not the little girl ("Lo-lee-ta: the tip of the tongue taking a trip of three steps down the palate to tap, at three, on the teeth. Lo. Lee. Ta.");[2] he dismissed "minor readers" as "those who identify with the characters." Imagination, memory, and the dictionary are, he told his students, the staples of the discerning reader.

You may also be interested to know that your fiction has by my unscientific culling of the *PMLA* bibliographies for the past six years spawned as many Ph.D. theses as anyone this side of Medieval and Neo-Latin Literature, which is to say in American and British literatures. I attribute this not only to the fecundity of ideas in your fiction but also to the questions of aesthetics and literary criticism it explicitly raises.

Shouldn't your insights into the writing of fiction be radical and disruptive enough for Mary McCarthy, who demands that ideas be juggled in full view of the reader? I may be somewhat obtuse myself, but I am also puzzled by the tendency of so

---

[1] François Truffaut, "Don't Bogart My Gauloises," *Toronto Life*, March 1978, p. 118.

[2] Vladimir Nabokov, *Lolita* (New York: Berkley, 1966), p. 11.

many readers to label the metaphysical configuration of your fiction as enervated or eviscerated. Molesworth, typical of many, has written, "To choose between, say, John Barth and S. Beckett, might be to choose between two exhaustions, two forms of fully articulated 'belatedness.' As we used to say back home, 'mighty slim pickins,' indeed."¹ That *Giles Goat-Boy* or *The Sot-Weed Factor* or *Letters* can be regarded as betraying exhaustion befuddles me – they are long, energetic, intricate: George Giles quests indomitably, Burlingame eats indomitably, Germaine and Ambrose copulate indomitably, you, I assume, write indomitably. You display all the delight that Borges does in humanity's contrivances, mechanical, physical, social, philosophical, theological, literary; because you and he don't believe they are anything except fiction does not reduce you and him to the status of *Endgame*'s Hamm and Clov.

My guess is that many readers have preconceptions about fiction that have become rigid, clichéd. If there are thirteen ways of looking at a blackbird, there is surely more than one way of writing and reading a novel, especially when that one way assumes so much about life and art. Must serious thematics, for instance, be treated seriously? What Randall Jarrell writes of the readers of contemporary poetry can be applied to the readers of the postmodern novel:

> When someone says, "I don't read modern poetry because it's all that stuff that nobody on earth can understand," I know enough to be able to answer, though not aloud: "It isn't; and, even if it were, *that's* not the reason you don't read it." The poet seems difficult *because* he is not read, *because* the reader is not accustomed to reading his or any other poetry.²

Your novels are misappropriated as nihilistic or obfuscatory or exhausted or are misinterpreted as being sterilely self-reflexive not because they are difficult, but because they are wilfully

---

¹ Charles Molesworth, "Reflections," *Salmagundi*, No. 50-51 (1980-81), p. 103.

² Randall Jarrell as quoted by John Wheatcroft in an unpublished paper entitled "Today's Poetry is Protest."

misread. This is done by those unwilling to relinquish their hold on the sacrosanct verities of the traditional novel and, indeed, the traditional world. Postmodernist fiction can be seen to be a literature of replenishment if, as you have said, readers are willing to keep one foot in "the narrative past" and one foot in "the Parisian structuralist present."[1] It is a good balancing act for a juggler, even Mary McCarthy's juggler, the meaning of which comes from jester, a legitimate and not to be eschewed or patronized stance, even when the ways we organize and inhabit our world are played with.

To the other tasks which I delineated in my preamble (prolix, prolix, I am Cooking with Gass): the Barth, -es, -elme connection is a remarkably apt one, the funhouse of language yoking the poststructuralist and postmodernist enterprises. Both ensconce fiction-making or constructing as seminal human activities and concomitantly elevate form above content; both devalue absolutes, and concepts such as self, origin, logos, idealism. As John Sturrock has written of the Parisian structuralist in the Barth, -es, -elme trinity, realism is his enemy; it "makes of literature the servant of reality because it holds the instrumental view of language; Realism presupposes that language is transparent, as it were, that 'through' words we look at life."[2] For you and -elme (see the way he deconstructs domes ticity in his story "Critique de la Vie Quotidienne") as well as for -es, life is no measurable, static entity but is itself a construct. As for the aforementioned Borges who is, I think, the model here, there is a delight in but not a belief in philosophical systems, notions of personal identity or cause and effect or continuity, etc. In addition, language is, as Sturrock contends, not an instrument, a transparent medium which can elucidate the "real" (here regarded as "constructed") world. In short, the world humanity has ordered and inhabits is appreciated *aesthetically*, which is to say, not literally. Like Giles, the nascent Grand Tutor, you, -es, and -elme apprehend the unreality, the fictiveness, of the real world:

---

[1] Barth, p. 70.

[2] John Sturrock, "Roland Barthes," in *Structuralism and Since*, ed. John Sturrock (Oxford: Oxford Univ. Press, 1979), p. 65.

Indeed, if I never came truly to despair at the awful
arbitrariness of Facts, it was because I never more than
notionally accepted them. *The Encyclopedia Tammanica* I
read from Aardvaark to Zymurgy in quite the same
spirit as I read the *Old School Tales*, my fancy prefacing
each entry "Once upon a time . . . . "[1]

There is a marked similarity between this perspective and that
winnowed from -es's *Mythologies*: -es operates on the everyday
dimensions of French life – wrestling, magazines, the Tour de
France bicycle race among others – and denaturalizes them; he
reveals that they are not ideologically neutral, not, in other
words, natural except by a kind of unconscious or quiescent
consensus. In his preface to *Mythologies* -es articulates this point,
which is yours as well: "The starting point of these reflections
was usually a feeling of impatience at the sight of the 'natural-
ness' with which newspapers, art and common sense constantly
dress up a reality which, even though it is the one we live in, is
undoubtedly determined by history."[2] So much postmodernist
literature, not only yours and -elme's, involves the denaturalizing of the "real" world: there is, for example, A.B. Paulson's
short story "The Minnesota Multiphasic Personality: a diagnostic test in two parts" which undermines the validity of the
Minnesota Multi-facet Personality Inventory. Paulson mimics
the format of the actual test, seducing the reader into believing
in its legitimacy (and by extension that of other such constructs)
until, perhaps, the following question: "8 T F I have not made
lewd faces at matrons descending excalators."[3]

Both the poststructuralists (e.g., -es) and the postmodernists
(e.g., you and -elme), denaturalize not only world but also text,
a paradox permissible because the hue and cry over your play
with these conventions is attributable to the reified status they

[1] John Barth, *Giles Goat-Boy or, The Revised New Syllabus* (New York: Fawcett, 1967), p. 117.

[2] Roland Barthes, *Mythologies*, trans. Annette Lavers (New York: Hill and Wang, 1972), p. 11.

[3] A.B. Paulson, "The Minnesota Multiphasic Personality: a diagnostic test in two parts," *Tri-Quarterly*, No. 29 (Winter 1974), p. 208.

have in the minds of advocates of the traditional novel. It was Sartre who said that a technique is already a metaphysic. You, -es, and -elme and also Derrida, whose work impinges on this issue especially, constantly expose the metaphysical aspects of what have become the rigidified and calcified conventions of fiction. Neither you nor -elme uses traditional devices unless you are intent on revealing the artifice inherent in them, as, for instance, you have done with the epistolary novel in *Letters*.

The term I would use to define the epistemological tendencies of you, -es, and -elme is ludic (from *ludere*, to play), since "playful" has somewhat pejorative or jejune connotations. The ludic sensibility is one which tends to see the structures that lie behind and determine reality, one which wants to discover and expose the roles of the various games people play. Johan Huizinga's *Homo Ludens* was the first major work to explore this motif. More recent theorists such as Jacques Ehrmann have even been more relentless than Huizinga was in establishing the ludic dimensions of culture: Ehrmann criticized Huizinga for his conclusion that games and culture are antithetical, the latter providing the yardstick for the former. Games in this context include, of course, not merely literal games but also the systems, codes, and abstracts which order the so-called real world. For Gass, for instance, philosophy and fiction are analogous games:

> They are divine games. Both play at gods as others play at bowls; for there is frequently more reality in fairy tales than in these magical constructions of the mind, works equally of thought and energy and will, which raise up into sense and feeling, as to life, acts of pure abstraction, passes logical, and intuitions both securely empty and as fitted for passage as time.[1]

Another witty and ludic aperçu of Gass's is that "the soul, we must remember, is the philosopher's invention, as thrilling a creation as, for instance, Madame Bovary."[2] Your whimsical

---

[1] William H. Gass, *Fiction and the Figures of Life* (New York: Knopf, 1970), p. 4.

[2] Gass, *Fiction and the Figures of Life*, p. 5.

comment that God wasn't a bad novelist, but s/he was a realist, provides another ludic perspective on art and life; it also coheres with the insight of contemporary "games" theorist Kostas Axelos, who has written, "Man is caught up in the game of the world. Playing on several levels. He and the game."[1]

The other definition of play that has affinities with your own is Derrida's. He writes:

> Play is the disruption of presence. The presence of an element is always a signifying and substitutive reference inscribed in a system of differences and the movement of a chain. Play is always play of absence and presence, but if it is to be thought radically, play must be conceived of before the alternative of presence and absence. Being must be conceived as presence or absence on the basis of the possibility of play and not the other way around.[2]

Because Derrida's theories destroy notions of origin, indeed, of a "real" world, his work has drawn the wrath of many critical theorists (Graff in *Literature Against Itself* and Hirsch in *The Aims of Interpretation* are two who come immediately to mind) who feel it unfairly and inaccurately undermines truth-claims in literature, literary criticism, and metaphysics. Certainly, the ludic sensibility *is* one which devalues absolutes of any kind. Masterworks such as *The Riddle of the Sphincters* which unearth "the mystery of the Universe" are presented in a parodic manner. Yet there is on the part of the ludic novelist a fascination with herculean, or what might be called Pynchonesque attempts to discern or create order in the universe. Thus, in *Letters* your convoluted histories of the Cook-Burlingame clan, Todd Andrews's obsession with recurrences, and the zeal with which Jacob Horner and Jerome Bray enumerate multifarious historical events. There is on the part of these characters and Reg Prinz and the Author a desire to

---

[1] Kostas Axelos, "Planetary Interlude," *Yale French Studies*, No. 41 (1968), p. 11.

[2] Jacques Derrida, *Writing and Difference*, trans. Alan Bass (Chicago: Univ. of Chicago Press, 1978), p. 292.

integrate seemingly diffuse world events as well as personal ones. As Ambrose says, "History is a code which, laboriously and at ruinous cost, deciphers into HISTORY. She is a scattered sybyl whose oak-leaf oracles we toil to recollect, only to spell out something less than nothing: e.g., WHOL TRUTH, or ULTIMATE MEANIN."[1] Straining like Oedipa Maas to confirm a Trystero system which would indicate that there is some trans-personal meaning, your characters yearn to see what Jacob Horner calls "the Big Picture, which you will likely Never See; or which, if it exists at all, may be like those messages spelled out at halftime in U.S. college football matches by marching undergraduates: less intelligent, valuable, and significant than its constituent units."[2] Reg Prinz's frantic attempts to capture it all in that most contemporary of media, the cinema, will fail to produce the Big Picture.

The configuration of your title, letters spelling what might be called the subtitle and making up the letters L-E-T-T-E-R-S, draws attention to another medium and its potential for con-joining the disparate doings of the world. Despite Bray's contention that " . . . B is the instrument of creation, the mother of letters and of the world Amen,"[3] "History's palindrome" cannot be set in type. Of Joyce's persuasion and appetite to write the world's meaning, you with your ludic temperament understand that "History's palindrome" is far too convoluted to be written, that there are only words, not "the direct, epileptic Word;" nonetheless, language is such a rich, malleable medium that you are fascinated by the attempt to create elaborate, labyrinthine funhouses out of it.

The postmodernists' canon is full of funhouse makers, of creators who want to rival "God the realist/novelist," who want to reinvent the world: for instance, your Author, Oedipa Maas, J. Henry Waugh, Jethro Furber, Cyril of *The Blood Oranges*. They state, along with the Voice in Coover's play

[1] John Barth, *Letters* (New York: Putnam's, 1970), p. 332.
[2] Barth, *Letters*, p. 404.
[3] Barth, *Letters*, p. 328.

"Love Scene," "Imagination rules the word, shithead!"[1] Formalists of the fantastic, they wish to fashion more intricate, more harmonious, and more aesthetically appealing games than the ones created for them, the ones they are forced to inhabit. Postmodernists might be called formalists of the fantastic for another reason. By denaturalizing reality they turn everyday experience into a fantastical thing. In *The Fantastic*, Todorov cites Sartre on the extraordinary quality of the mundane:

There is now only one fantastic object: man. Not the man of religions and spiritualisms, only half committed to the world of the body, but man-as-given, man-as-nature, man-as-society, the man who takes off his hat when a hearse passes, who kneels in churches, who marches behind a flag.[2]

It is insofar as their actions reflect or have assimilated *les règles du jeu*, the rules of the game, which are not natural, that people are fantastic to postmodernists. For Sartre the fantastic is a matter of content; for the postmodernists it is a matter of form.

---

[1] Robert Coover, *A Theological Position* (New York: Dutton, 1972), p. 98.

[2] Tzvetan Todorov, *The Fantastic: A Structural Approach to a Literary Genre* (Cleveland: Press of Case Western Reserve Univ., 1973), p. 173.

CULTURE

Travels With My Cant

ARE YOU TATTOOED, JACQUES DERRIDA?

Tattoos are supposed to be for sailors, members of motorcycle gangs, toughs, the occasional hooker (her buttocks, perhaps, butterflied). Crowns, anchors, daggers, roses, and crosses comprise their kitschy art – mostly advertising mom or unreasonable facsimiles thereof. Have you met any lawyers lately with "nolo contendere" etched on their biceps or doctors with the Hippocratic oath reversed on their chests for easily mirrored recall? And, though some *de rigueur* sociologist has probably produced "Tattoo Practices of East Coast Longshoremen, 1921-37," have you known any academics who have put their macho where their mouths are in the shape of their university's crest and motto? Come to think of it, how many of you readers out there are simpatico with seafarers?

I have been speculating in this way recently because not too long ago I was in a Thailand tattoo parlour debating on the appropriate image in red and blue which would frame the word "Entropy," providing my frame with its (un)fashionably arcane imprimatur. Why would I do this, it might be asked. I wear no jewellery – no ring or necklace, not even a watch. Tattoos draw me less for their intrinsic attractions than their gestural properties. The persona Bruce Dern plays in *Tattoo* elevates his work to the status of art and religion, but that's too profound (the gesture, not the movie) for my temperament and taste. Entropy, with its connotations of randomness and diffuse energy, might seem to indicate nihilism or despair; I don't feel either of these

127

things inordinately, though. No, the word was chosen more because if one wants a tattoo, one has to have something to tattoo and entropy is a frequent literary motif in contemporary literature. (It is more enduring probably than many of the loves who have been immortalized in the flesh.)

Acquiring the tattoo, simply put, was more important than its particular mark, medium here emphasized over message. Yet the medium has its own message and in this case can be appreciated best by means of the following anecdote: I was to give a paper at a scholarly conference together with one of Canada's pre-eminent writers, Robert Kroetsch. Before Kroetsch arrived a conferee approached me and said, "Oh, you must be Robert Kroetsch," presumably because in blue jeans and T-shirt I looked unlike an academic, like a poet. Soon after, Kroetsch appeared, impeccably dressed.

Even in demotic North America professors wear their titles and degrees more proudly than sailors their superbly crafted "skull and bones." Also, insouciant dress is thought to belong most properly to the bohemian poet rather than the institutional academic. The former can be unshaven, tattooed; the latter should be tonsured, circumspect. Art, in this formulation, is a disruptive entity; thus the artist can be outlandish. Literary criticism, on the other hand, is regarded as an explanatory act and the critic as conservative. The former forges a tradition, which is to say, first alters it; the latter preserves a tradition, enshrines it.

Recently, however, a challenge to this order has emerged via deconstruction. Its devotees, rejecting the critical acts of explanation and conservation, are the tattooed intruders in the sherry-party atmosphere of faculty clubs. The *critical* act as the disruptive act? The hallowed tradition some people's fictions? Culture's privileged place a sham? My, my, it's no wonder that some patrician academics squirm. The maîtres d' will lose their prestigious faculty club positions to tattoo artists, gentility will give way to beer brawls, and anarchy will overrun Western civilization.

THE UBIQUITOUS CANADIAN

Imagine an idyll on one of Fiji's exotic, sun-splashed outer islands – lush tropical blossoms, stunning white sand, a bountiful ocean glazed turquoise, bures (thatched huts) to domicile you simply but charmingly. What enchanting sounds waft through the snug, humid, un-Canadian air? Chances are they will have their source not only in the poetry-producing and -inducing throat of an indigenous bird but also in the glottis of the Canadian version of a "good old boy," a Bob and Doug McKenzie clone, doing his ersatz version of the Great White North shtick. Canada meets the South Pacific, and greets it with a "co roo-coo-coo" and a blind drunk. You can take someone out of Moose Jaw, Saskatchewan, or The Brunswick House bar in Toronto but not, it appears, vice versa.

Every place, to begin again, this time a little more generally and perhaps a little more charitably, is somebody's Florida. What should be realized is that travel agents have become the new pop fiction makers. Their craft is similar to the novelist's – invent a world that only incidentally, tangentially (if not irrelevantly) matches the real one. Their only criterion is that their world be alluring. However, inhabiting the thaumaturgic forest of W.H. Hudson's *Green Mansions* or the sensuous Illyria of John Hawkes's *The Blood Oranges*, one is certain not to confront the ubiquitous Canadian or any of many other equally noxious, unedenic intrusions. The Seychelles may host the world's Rotarians and Baja California may be the scene of the next world dune buggy championships; Rima and Cyril, of the above-mentioned novels, though, romping on their terrains, will never face such disturbances.

All of this isn't meant to deter you from a jaunt to the South Pacific or elsewhere. Certainly, it is a lot warmer in Fiji than it is in Canada; also, the reverse motion of water draining in your sink or bathtub will captivate you for days. Still, if you wish to enhance your junket, to keep the prairies and your paradise separate, the following travel tips are offered:

* never place a Canadian flag or other such logo on your suitcase;

* visit countries where English is little known by their citizenry;
* further, try to find those in which the script is unrecognizable to you;
* wear lederhosen, dashikis, caftans, or sulus;
* when addressed in English, say "je regrette," "vas?" or "maaf kan saya."

MINIMALISM

A dominant impression of cities of the Far East: hawkers, sellers, traders, trinkets, swatches, watches. In Singapore grave men, looking sage and astute enough to manage countries and economies, sit at the front of their well-stocked shops, goods piled behind them in precise, Mondrian-like patterns. Who makes these goods and are there enough buyers for them? In Bangkok, with a more tenuous hold, literally and metaphorically, on material security, people squat on the pavement spreading objects for sale on mats or towels.

And what of our more expansive, perhaps, Western establishments, not to mention the yard sales, mail-order catalogues, and Amway dealers – products and blandishments that seep (more subtly but no less insistently) into the house like asbestos fibres? The horror, the horror. The Gross (?) National Product defines a country's well-being, its bounty. "Make more, buy more" is the prevailing maxim.

Approximately 130 years ago, Henry David Thoreau left Concord, Mass., for a few years at his Walden retreat. Not a misanthropist, he did this, he affirmed, to discover what was essential for the good life. Not much, he muttered in so many words. Then with "Simplify, Simplify" echoing throughout his book, *Walden*, he launched into diatribes against most of the much that littered his pre-Woolco (this is not to exclude Piaget, Gucci, etc.) world. Thoreau had his sixties renaissance as a dissenter and pastoralist, the duty of being disobedient obviously being paramount in the Vietnam war era.

He deserves another curtain call now, this time as the

avatar of minimalism, which might be called the intellectual equivalent of silence. Fastidious Thoreau would have been horrified at excess baggage stuffing the bellies of planes, the bellies and minds of people; he would have recoiled at pavement littered with stools – in both senses of the word. Not a Luddite, he nonetheless considered much that humanity makes as excrescences of various kinds.

Thoreau's prescription, it should be noted, does not advocate the kind of cultism in which the Oregon swami and other "I want to be God" gurus urge their underlings to give up their baggage – to them. It simply demands a ruthless stock-taking which would render the Dow-Jones nearly superfluous.

In a contemporary rendition of the virtues of minimalism and silence, William Gass writes of a supreme fantasy in which all courts, clubs, and stadia are closed, magazines are unmailed, and publishers "issue no more dick, prick and booby books."

"Fewer goods, less junk" is the noble goal here. However, what will people do with such space, such silence? Aren't rooms to be filled, vacuums (except Hoover's) to be abhorred? Isn't the spate of magazines, movies, TV channels, TVs, among many other things, necessary if not because those things provide choices, but because they provide work, business (busy-ness)? Well, Thoreau's years at Walden were a paean to idleness as much as anything else. No ballgames to listen to, only one skimpy book to write – what did that delinquent man do with his time?

WHEN IS A HOOKER NOT A HOOKER?

Disclaimer: This research was in no way sponsored by the Canada Council, Fulbright, or other such august bodies (though with the proper academic veneer – footnotes and graphs – it would probably fly). Delineated herein are the investigations and observations of a naif – not in the bumbling adolescent sense of a Tom Jones, but in the sense of an untutored visitor to another world, as it were.

Those of you hardened (unfortunate pun, perhaps) by prostitution, North American style, would be stripped (ah, the magical life language leads within itself, to quote John Updike) of your defences in Thailand. For the women of whom I write ooze (oops) yearning, goodwill, and, almost beyond one's ken, desire of all things – not an automaton among them, not a clockwatcher, yawner (ahem), idler.

Collectively shudder, please, to think how such a style would fare on Sunset Blvd. in Los Angeles, for instance, where alluring exterior gives way to life-size inflatable doll once the fare's been paid – alas, before the meter begins to run its remote (coarse) course. No, in bar upon bar upon bar stocked with the girls of Thailand – an industry more finely tuned than that in the Toyota plants – bottles cry for their corks (that's Pope, this time – Alexander, to be sure) not only shrilly but also whole-heartedly, feelingly.

Moreover, once the match is made, mere mechanics remain subordinated to ambience. What you get rather peremptorily is a girlfriend with all that entails – handholding, dinner, strolling, shopping, affection. It's as if the Chamber of Commerce were embodied in their bodies. You might even get some of the less sanguine trappings of courtship such as jealousy and petulance; these, however, appear to be more than compensated for.

It is no wonder, then, that – say it starkly – Thailand's number one import is surely jism (which is quickly exported – ha, ha). Japanese businessmen, with their yen and their yen bulked by the exchange rate, flood the streets. Also many Germans girdled by girth and their economic miracle – the two seem in tandem everywhere – amble contentedly with their marks.

Thai women are, of course, baht (that, for the sake of language play, is the Thai currency) and sold. (There are even seamier sanctioned practices easily available, too, as there are all around the world, no doubt.) What Bangkok and environs parade, though, is fellow-feeling in the persons of concubines. The atmosphere is neither jaded nor decadent – callousness and boredom are not in evidence. Wholesomeness radiates – it's a high school prom of the streets and sheets.

It's a variation on a theme. The women seem to be audition-ing for *Apocalypse Now*, the Vietnam war cruelly removing every Charlie from his midwestern "Park and Eat" so he can be coddled abroad.

CLICHÉS AND THE TRAVELLER

Once in Thailand I was called (not by a Thai) a bloody German; another time I was asked if I were a member of a visiting German soccer team. Travel, which is said to be broadening and enlightening, can also cause one to be straitjacketed in national stereotypes. Individual characteristics are easily transposed into counters redolent of national significance.

Everyone, I think, is susceptible to such processes. For instance, I noticed that many Japanese handled their cigarette lighters in such a way, flourishing them as valued, dependable objects, that I thought it no wonder their expertise in and mastery of things technological. The reverence for a product as product, its internal wonders and workings, renders its social or cultural impact secondary.

Similarly, the way the "underprivileged" citizens of Bangkok and Singapore relished their cigarettes, inhaling not toxic substances but substance, bespeaks their desire for goods, for material things, the way middle class children exult over newly acquired video games or Beverly Hills matrons their bodies after breast implants. And what of the frantic manoeuvrings of car and motorcycle drivers in Asian cities? Surely it represents their struggle for some modest space amidst the teeming cities. More global implications can be drawn. Faulkner writing of "the same frantic steeplechase to nowhere everywhere" draws in the denizens of New York and Waterloo, Ont., as well as Bangkok. Literature, especially, moves like this from Joyce's Dublin and Robert Kroetsch's Alberta to nowhere everywhere.

That movement, though, is less pronounced for the traveller. Places are appreciated and assessed for the ways they reflect national tendencies. Travelling is a selfish act: Show me your characteristics, your uniqueness, citizen(ry). Thus, the urge to travel to hitherto xenophobic China, to collect its passport stamp, an indigenously Chinese mark or experience – the way baseball card collectors want the whole set, especially including the rarest cards in the collection. This validates one's travels. Wats are different from churches, bahts from dollars, wais from handshakes – Kodak capturing these and other distinctions. The process works reciprocally: one is first and foremost what one's passport says one is, complete with fixed impressions and stereotypical baggage.

If such a world view is not maintained, think of the consequences for Canadian nationalists, for example. There *is* a Canadian character, a Canadian experience, a Canadian legacy that is of paramount importance. National character, though, is not an uncritical good. Presently, if I am correct, it operates too oppressively as the framework for travel, for the collection and definition of exotic experiences. Kurt Vonnegut has written of what he whimsically calls "granfalloons," those agencies of false bonding that link people arbitrarily. Being Canadian means you drive on the opposite side of the road than your Thai counterpart and have access to more TV channels. Is invoking a national stereotype to accentuate further differences to be valued much?

Emily Dickinson rarely left the community, indeed, the house, in which she was raised, yet her poetry takes one into fantastical territory; the average science fiction writer, Michel Butor writes, creates monsters more banal than your next door neighbour. All this is to say that travel, given its nationalistic contexts, is often narrowing rather than liberating and also that most fantastical realms are products of *language* – language used in an imaginative, not a clichéd way.

OF CEREMONY AND CIVILIZATION

It would be foolish to try to supplant Roland Barthes's *Empire of Signs* and it is to that book one should go to gain insight into the uniquely ceremonial nature of Japan. Nonetheless, despite Barthes's pellucid prose, his work presents some difficulties to those unfamiliar with his methodology; a restatement with a few individually drawn examples is not, I think, inappropriate.

Barthes's fascination with Japan centres mainly on that culture's recognition of the seminal role of signs, of ceremony. Contrary to this is what Western civilization tends to prize: the natural, the realistic. "Be yourself," say the pop psychologists; "how true to life," say the unsophisticated moviegoers. Such folk do not realize the important, intractable media through which self and art make their impact; they are unaware that our concepts of "natural" and "realistic" are heavily coded, that, to speak of the second term, realism is only one of many literary conventions.

Barthes celebrates all those facets of Japanese life that do not mask their artifice, that is to say that acknowledge their masks: kabuki theatre, for instance, with its stylized fight sequences, its stage assistants dressed in black and considered invisible, etc. Then there is sumo wrestling, which is as much Shinto ritualism as it is sport. The bunraku puppets, sushi bars, tea ceremonies – these and many other aspects of Japanese life manifest their ceremonial natures even before their explicit purposes (the puppets for entertainment, the sushi for nourishment, the tea for drinking).

Art and sport in other Eastern countries are also enmeshed in such rituals. Thai dancing with its elaborate head-dresses and elongated nails comes to mind. So, too, does Thai boxing which despite its affinities with the more widely recognized mode of boxing is preceded by protracted, demanded religious gestures.

It is true, of course, that ceremony has its role in Western culture. Where it is not apparent is in the realm of politics, where the trappings of ceremony clash so comically (and poignantly) with the jousting bit players. At the time I am writing this, the Queen of England, bagged and hatted as ever, is drawing gawking and adoring throngs, this time in California. Baseball, too, has its rituals which are largely unrecognized as such: formulaic manager-umpire arguments and the chewing of tobacco are peculiar to baseball and its hallowed tradition.

Clearly, though, in the West ceremony is either spectacle or assimilated behaviour. Ceremony has lost or never had the magical and ennobling properties it appears to have in the East, especially in Japan.

THE NEW YORKER VS. MY SLIDES

"There I am in front of the Sydney Opera House . . . and there disappearing under an avalanche of bar girls . . . and there at Emperor Hirohito's place – well, near it anyway . . . . " Are you yawning yet, already narcotized to the inevitable: Stanley's trip in picture and story? Does it make its impact the way others' dreams do on me? ("I dreamt I witnessed my conception while I was hang-gliding . . . . ")

Surely Kodak could save everyone the time and have mock-ups of the shrine of your choice (pyramids, Eiffel Tower, Raffles Hotel) in every 7-Eleven. When I show you mine, you could show me yours and the equilibrium of our relationship could be maintained.

There are two issues here. The first is the infernal but omnipresent camera. Already Susan Sontag in *On Photography* has written incisively about the photograph's growing hegemony over experience. Saying something is as pretty as a picture or asserting your photograph has captured the intended object or event lends credence to the uncritically held assumption that a photograph of anything is truer than, say, a written account of it.

Certainly, the camera makes different demands on the user than the pen does. (I'll say! I frequently left the bloody lens cover on – altered my settings incorrectly – forgot, after all that, to get my rolls of film out of my bag so that they wouldn't be zapped in Hong Kong's carnivorous X-ray equipment.)

The camera insists, for one, on distancing users immediately, forcing them to separate themselves from what they wish to photograph and to do so as soon as the opportunity occurs. Writing, on the other hand, is most often pursued reflectively, allowing for both participation and observation. Its devaluation in comparison with film and photography produces another deleterious consequence: the latter two, except in the hands of experimental cineasts and photographers, deflect an awareness of the medium. They urge the viewer to believe ("seeing is believing") that the lens is irrefutable. (Antonioni's movie, *Blow-Up*, comes to mind as a work which tries to undermine such a facile perception.)

The second issue is the stature of the traveller's stories (filmed or otherwise). It's an urgent concern as I am being hurried homeward at this moment. Will my response to "How was your trip?" send my friends into a stupor? *The New Yorker* gets away with stating the banal, the trivial. Recently, their reporter-at-large intrepidly proceeded to regale his readers with the minutiae of his Brussels to Paris train trip: when it left (exactly) and arrived (ditto), where he sat, what he ate, etc. In the same issue thirty or so pages are devoted to a meticulous profile of Ponce Cruse Evans, the author of "Hints from Heloise." (Bet you're all breathless to discover whether her pinkie lands on her teacup when she drinks.)

How is it *The New Yorker* can pass on trivial impressions and discoveries and either not render you comatose and take your money or render you comatose and still take your money? Most likely it is the glossy or sophisticated context in which such communication takes place. After all, haven't you read me this far?

ENDLESS LOVE

I am inured to seeing the television screen littered with the salvation-donation hysterics of the fundamentalist set. The craggy-faced, gesticulating, portentous guy who was uttering his earnest imprecations about love to his simpering audience, video's answer to canned laughter, was, I assumed, another of that eschatological ilk. As it turned out he was Leo Buscaglia – don't forget the status-inflating "Dr.", as you wouldn't omit the similar puffery of "Rev." Ken Campbell. Buscaglia, author of a number of best-sellers (such is the state of mass culture) and from my vantage point metaphorical layer-on of hands, told heartfelt anecdotes about "sensitive" but "blocked" folks who just can't seem to "relate" or "share." In his vocal accompaniment to *Love Boat* he declaimed maxims echoed in his "how-to" books, which make the cynic recall Nabokov's witticism that the word cosmic is always in danger of losing its "s." His sententious phrases were uttered with all the sureness that, instead of fatuities, they were insights never before profferred. Moreover, those people who wouldn't think of shelling out ten bucks for a prayer hankie or a "Jesus Jukes" bumper sticker willingly, even respectfully, let Leo's shlock seep in and clog their mental pores; his books are displayed prominently, no doubt, on their coffee tables.

Especially in a pragmatic, materialistic age the fact that sentimentality flourishes could provoke surprise. The sixties may be passé politically (shame!) but a sanitized version of Woodstock and the Esalen Institute has continued to bulk love, propagating the notion that there is nothing holier than holistic behaviour. The malaise extends far beyond Buscaglia's burblings, which in a way is a pity because flaying him and his minions makes for ruddy sport. Love, after all, is a nominalist term, i.e., one that doesn't have any intrinsic or essential properties; those are attached by pop culture and such "experts" as Buscaglia, Michael Jackson, and the producers of the "soaps."

Sane, sophisticated people, bright and witty, our friends even, who can only guffaw at the thought of a Ronald Reagan or a Bill Vander Zalm shaping social policy, who relish nouvelle cuisine, disdain Hollywood films, and are sceptical of most other nominalist terms, lapse into mawkish, clichéd ways when (a) they fall madly in love, (b) their partners aren't being "real," (c) love's course doesn't run smooth, (d) et cetera. Vocabularies become redolent of "significance" and irony is obliterated. Rarely does one hear the kind of comment provided by cartoonist Lynda Barry when she said relationships and love play too great a role in women's lives. Even the personal advertisements in *The New York Review of Books* – always on the leading edge – have become domesticated, cloying. They are rife with calls for "commitment," "responsibility," "nurturing," and the search for permanence, a far cry, indeed, from those marvellous *Berkeley Barb* or *Georgia Strait* ads of ten or fifteen years ago in which Taurus females sought Pisces males or vice versa for "a big feed" or other such non-enduring pleasures.

Although he himself was overly preoccupied with meaningful relationships, D.H. Lawrence wrote a poem "The Mess of Love" in which he averred,

We've made a great mess of love
since we made an ideal of it.
The moment I swear to love a woman, a certain woman,
all my life that moment

I begin to hate her.
The moment I even say to a woman: I love you!
my love dies down considerably.[1]

To deflate "love" demands an intellectual enema, an evacuation of romance and its accretions. Yet nowhere does one encounter sceptical or even frivolous commentators who offer an antidote to Buscaglia and the rest of the sincere-heartfelt crew that inflates love endlessly. What is required is, quite simply, the deconstruction of love, that is to say the recognition that it is a concept that has been over-inflated, over-valued. Treacle about "love" has trickled unabated into all social and emotional arenas. Otherwise how does one explain the utterly credulous response to Buscaglia by those who gag at Falwell on the family or at other unsophisticated formulations?

Perhaps pop psychologists and the whole "how-to" network are to blame. One countervailing perspective can be found in some contemporary poetry, in the writing of Gregory Corso, for example, who mediates wittily on romantic topics, never giving in to the facile or the overly sentimental. To quote Corso in a poem on marriage,

I never wanted to marry a girl who was like my mother
And Ingrid Bergman was always impossible
And there's maybe a girl now but she's already married
And I don't like men and – [2]

---

[1] D.H. Lawrence, "The Mess of Love," in *D.H. Lawrence: The Poems*, eds. Vivian de Sola Pinto and F. Warren Robarts (New York: Penguin, 1977), p. 472.

[2] Gregory Corso, "Marriage," in *The Norton Anthology of Modern Poetry*, eds. Richard Ellmann and Robert O'Clair (New York: W.W. Norton, 1973), p. 1259.

CONCLUSION

Def(y)ning Postmodernism

"The professor is someone who finishes his sentences,"[1] writes Barthes. Contrarily, lucidly, Barthes sought to undo the sanctity of the professoriat, writing a good many complete sentences, but not too many "well developed" tomes. Aphorisms, fragments, alphabetically structured *jeux d'esprit* – these were among the manoeuvres deployed by Barthes to deny closure and definition, or to write them ironically. Of himself in *Roland Barthes* he writes, " . . . he doesn't like the ends: the risk of the rhetorical clausule is too great: the fear of not being able to resist the *last word*."[2] Writing in the third person, he renders himself fictive, distancing himself from sincerity, from disclosure (except as dis-closure). To define postmodernism requires such perversity (Barthes's favourite word in *The Pleasure of the Text*): the heightened self-consciousness it fosters generates a sensibility that resists compartmentalization. If, as Barthes speculates, to name is to neutralize, transforming postmodern heterogeneity, contrariety, into an "ism" truncates it in the act of incorporating it. Nonetheless (and perversely) the academic reification of postmodernism does provide some destablization of the boundaries of literature and literary criticism, for instance, by demanding "author" status for Kathy Acker, whose plagiarizing, "cuntaminating"[3] art is the intellectual equivalent of slam-dancing. One should, however, always have in mind

---

[1] Roland Barthes, *The Pleasure of the Text*, trans. Richard Miller (New York: Hill and Wang, 1975), p. 50.

[2] Ronald Barthes, *Roland Barthes*, trans. Richard Howard (New York: Hill and Wang, 1977), p. 94.

[3] The term is coined by Jane Gallop in *The Daughter's Seduction: Feminism and Psychoanalysis* (Ithaca, N.Y.: Cornell Univ. Press, 1982), p. 31.

the scene in Ginsberg's *Howl* in which his beloved outcasts, "the best minds" of his generation, "threw potato salad at CCNY lecturers on Dadaism."[1] In this situation, should you try to duplicate the feat, you will only stain some pages. I will, though, endeavour to reduce my authority whenever I am called upon to explain the postmodern sensibility. I promise.

M. Gilbert Porter notwithstanding (see "Introduction"), superficiality is a prized postmodern characteristic, what Fredric Jameson in "Postmodernism, or The Cultural Logic of Late Capitalism" calls its supreme formal feature. Although Jameson's comments concern architecture primarily, they can be extrapolated to encompass, especially, fiction and literary theory. Here, the end of humanism with its notion of a self as ontologically solid, as profoundly deep, is proclaimed. Foucault, of course, is the one who has written this eradication most insistently. In the conclusion to *The Order of Things* he argues that " . . . man is neither the oldest nor the most constant problem that has been posed for human knowledge"; moreover, "a change in the fundamental arrangements of knowledge,"[2] not some intrinsic, essential elements, validated him. For Foucault a further shift in the paradigms for the production of knowledge will spell his dissolution. Barthelme, among other writers of fiction, also tenaciously, if comically, offers the dispersion of self, and a scepticism towards subjectivity and towards a self that is present to itself. In "Daumier" he lists Daumier's readings on the self, a group of works that in their diversity of focuses provides an ironic commentary on the status of the "I":

> *The Self: An Introduction* by Meyers, *Self-Abuse* by Samuels, *The Armed Self* by Crawlie, Burt's *The Concept of Self, Self-Congratulation* by McFee, Fingarette's *Self-Deception, Self-Defence for Women and Young Girls* by Birch, Winterman's *Self-Doubt, The Effaced Self* by Lilly,

---

[1] Allen Ginsberg, *Howl and Other Poems* (San Francisco: City Lights, 1956), p. 15.

[2] Michel Foucault, *The Order of Things: An Archeology of the Human Sciences* (New York: Vintage, 1973), pp. 386-87.

CONCLUSION

Self-Hatred in Vermin by Skinner, Le Bett's *Selfishness*, Gordon's *Self-Love* ... Hickel's *Self-Propelled Vehicles* ....[1]

Appropriating a remark of one of Barthelme's characters, the self and its dilemmas, authentication, etc. are common knowledge, so common in fact they may not even be true.

A grounded self, a self that is present to itself, one that is not constituted by social codes and linguistic conventions, gets no reinforcement whatsoever from postmodern writers. Concomitantly, there is in postmodern art a waning of affect, another attribute cited by Jameson.[2] With no identification with the characters possible (the roster of postmodern characters including Pynchon's Genghis Cohen and Stanley Koteks, Barthelme's Hogo de Bergerac and Jane Villiers de l'Isle Adam), epistemological rather than ethical problems become prominent. Daumier's description of Celeste, for example, deploys metaphor in order to engage questions about metaphor rather than to present Celeste more distinctively:

> ... the legs on her were as long and slim as his hope of Heaven and the thighs on her were as strong and sweet-shaped as ampersands and the buttocks on her were as pretty as two pictures and the waist on her was as neat and incurved as the waist of a fiddle and the shoulders on her were as tempting as sex crimes and the hair on her was as long and black as Lent and the movement of the whole was honey ....[3]

Graff, one of postmodernism's most oft-heard critics (from the "right" that is, the left having its own "shtick"), complains relentlessly about the devaluation of and lack of sympathy for the bourgeois self, urging its re-establishment after a long

---

[1] Donald Barthelme, *Sadness* (New York: Pocket Books, 1980), p. 145.

[2] Fredric Jameson, "Postmodernism, or The Cultural Logic of Late Capitalism," *New Left Review*, No. 146 (July-Aug. 1984), p. 61.

[3] Barthelme, p. 171.

period of denigration. Indeed, one might accede to such a reversal – but only ironically, the way Barthes, after defending and extolling the avant-garde, suddenly turns around and revalues classical literature.

Another dimension of the postmodern sensibility might be called nominalist, expressing dubiousness regarding abstracts, absolutes, or essences. Knowledge for Foucault becomes knowledge-power, an ideological, historically conditioned knowledge produced, categorized, and controlled by experts. Our disciplines and taxonomies (as we saw in "Michel Foucault's Touchstones"), the framework of our universities (as we saw in "Intellectual Enemas"), the authority of the author (as we saw in "Gobble, Gobble, Gobble: Critical Appetites") – these are undercut, their statuses mitigated, attenuated. In *The Pleasure of the Text* Barthes constructs "a typology of the pleasures of reading – or of the readers of pleasure,"[1] dividing readers into fetishists, obsessives, paranoiacs, and hysterics. These categories yield a patina of authenticity, so used are we to having sages order and reorder the sprawling profusion of things. On the contrary, this schematizing of readers is an example of Barthes's whimsy as it extends to, or rather luxuriates in, concepts, ideas, theoretical speculations. By means of his taxonomies and neologisms (themselves ironically contextualized by Barthes off-handedly commenting, "Were we fond of neologisms . . . "), Barthes invents intellectual frameworks which manifest their fictive yet plausible character, similar to a novelist's creation of literary characters saturated with verisimilitude.

Eagleton's project in *Literary Theory: An Introduction* is relevant here, literature and literary criticism being regarded as arbitrarily and professionally created rather than intrinsically revealed and enshrined. Recently, I gave a lecture at the Royal Military College in Kingston, Ontario; I opted for the title "*Deacon*struction (sic)" to draw attention to the hagiographical, inflated nature of the critical enterprise. "Deacon," I discovered while preparing the address, is not only a noun (with the meaning in common use) but also a transitive verb with the following meanings: "to pack (vegetables or fruit) with only the

---

[1] Barthes, *The Pleasure of the Text*, p. 63.

finest pieces or the most attractive sides visible"; "to falsify (something), doctor"; "to castrate (a pig or other animal)."[1] Academic deacons deacon texts, providing literary packaging that advertises cultural and aesthetic needs and their assuaging, doctoring a little here, cutting a little there.

The palinode is another dimension of the postmodern project (see "Palinodes and Palindromes"). Anti-affirmative art and criticism, paradoxical rather than productive, and anti-teleological texts have become the objective. Coover, in celebrating Beckett in an essay called "The Last Quixote," writes that Beckett offered him "a way of going on, of making art, without affirmation; he guided me when Christ and Tennessee Williams failed . . . ."[2] Theological and aesthetic directions and definitions are abandoned. Novels such as Kathy Acker's *Great Expectations* deliberately refer to a work that they then attempt to unwrite. Deconstructive or postmodern critics, too, seek to provide texts which are the equivalent of the statement "this statement is false," cancelling instead of creating meanings. Lyotard's suspicion of metanarratives, of anything except ludic manoeuvres, becomes an attractive trait. In *The Daughter's Seduction,* for instance, Jane Gallop plays feminism off against psychoanalysis until neither is a winner/both are winners. In her text Gallop uses a double columnar method to present palinodic perspectives.

Postmodernism's most often used mode of reduction, deflation, or retraction is parody. As Molesworth defined it in *Donald Barthelme's Fiction: The Ironist Saved From Drowning*, parody in the postmodern vein is free floating; it is not used merely as a weapon to ridicule some excess, deviation, or aberration. Barthelme and Barthes incessantly parody their own most recent literary gestures which themselves become liable to parody. Linda Hutcheon's *A Theory of Parody* meticulously examines this infinitely self-referential style; there she traces Bakhtin's influence on the re-definition of parody, calling it "a

---

[1] From *The Random House Dictionary of the English Language*, 1973.

[2] Robert Coover, "The Last Quixote: Marginal Notes on the Gospel According to Samuel Beckett," *New American Review*, No. 11 (New York: Simon & Schuster, 1971), p. 136.

relativizing, deprivileging mode," one of the "techniques of self-referentiality by which art reveals its awareness of the context-dependent nature of meaning."[1] Again, Barthes's *Roland Barthes* provides the finest example of this kind of play.

One final postmodern quality, my own equivalent to Derrida's "différance," is miscegenation. In *The Daughter's Seduction* Gallop links etymologically the words "theory" and "theatre." She also "cuntaminates" her critical discourse to avoid nomination or definition. Impropriety, unfaithfulness, promiscuity, excess of interpretation – these are miscegenating ploys used by Gallop for whom "any discourse phallicizes . . . . "[2] She employs postmodern practices for feminist ends, writing the dispersion of patriarchal authority, of phallogocentrism. In *The Daughter's Seduction* she is always adulterating categories and proprieties: Lacanian terminology is mixed with baby talk, explication with punning, intricacy with frippery. Such subversion, such denial of what for Lyotard is the solace of good forms, is echoed by Irigaray, for whom, in *This Sex Which Is Not One*, the title stressing polyvocality, *glissement*, etc., a postmodern writing of woman does not allow for recuperable meanings. This project "put the torch to fetish words, proper terms, well-constructed forms."[3] Both Irigaray and Gallop champion and use a fluid style which "resists and explodes every firmly established form, figure, idea or concept."[4] Avoiding the production of hegemonic truths, of fixed meanings, demands a miscegenating that leaves no literary, critical, or social convention pristine, uncontaminated, pure. If for Robert Scholes in *Structuralism in Literature* marriage and structuralism are yoked, reconciling opposites, dyadic terms, then postmodernism rejects such neat forms of harmony and closure.

In this element of postmodernism, as in the others enunciated above, the scene of teaching and the act of criticism are

---

[1] Linda Hutcheon, *A Theory of Parody: The Teachings of Twentieth-Century Art Forms* (New York: Methuen, 1985), pp. 69, 85.

[2] Gallop, p. 125.

[3] Luce Irigaray, *This Sex Which Is Not One*, trans. Catherine Porter with Carolyn Burke (Ithaca, N.Y.: Cornell Univ. Press, 1985), p. 79.

[4] Irigaray, p. 79.

implicated. The consequences of such a refusal to frame literary studies, to make them a subject of disinterested study, have been pursued in "Intellectual Enemas" (as well as in a spate of other works). Nonetheless, they provide one of post-modernism's most distinctive operational aspects and deserve more exploration. Whereas the spokespersons for modernism in its shaping and codification were outside the academy, those who preside over the coalescing of postmodernism, via its critical-theoretical arm, deconstruction, as well as its "creative" one, speak from within universities. Thus the framing and valuing of postmodernism become an enterprise with academic consequences. For Graff and others on the so-called "right" the proclamation of humanism's death-knell demands countervailing pressure to rejuvenate the bourgeoisie as well as traditional humanistic practices. For those on the so-called "left" post-modernism is neo-conservative play, *mise en abyme*, that provides no ground from which to produce meaningful social change. Still others, advocates of deconstruction, seek to centre its discovery, desiring academia's imprimatur of respectability.

In his essay in *The Anti-Aesthetic*, "Opponents, Audiences, Constituencies and Community," Said contends that post-modernism as a centripetal academic activity becomes an ally of Reaganism. For Said, as long as literary criticism remains "only" literary criticism, it is doomed to be an eviscerated product. Although this is one of many readings of post-modernism, and despite all readings being misreadings, Said's remarks are apposite as postmodernism continues to grow as a field of study. A typographical error in his essay spawns the neologism "predagogues" (from pedagogues). Derrida, citing Nietzsche's comment that students are preyed upon, connected to the university by the ear, dangled by "the umbilical cord of the university," writes that this "links you, like a leash in the form of an umbilical cord, to the paternal belly of the State. Your pen is its pen; you hold its teleprinter as you hold those ballpoints in the post office which are attached to chains."[1] Unless the kind of miscegenation that will see academe's

---

[1] Jacques Derrida, "All Ears: Nietzsche's Otobiography," *Yale French Studies*, No. 63 (1982), p. 248.

discourse modified, resituated, and redirected occurs, Said's fears will have been realized; postmodernism will have offered a chance for a new "ism" to be domesticated into giving "good notes" and bulking a few resumés.